M000207421

"Two decades and one pandemic into a religious reality dramatically changed by digital technologies, social media, and the new modes of communications they have prompted, Ryan Panzer's *The Holy and the Hybrid* advances an essential conversation for church leaders and communities responding to the ministry needs of the digitally integrated world. Not only an important exploration of communication practices required for meaningful ministry engagement today, but also a guide to innovative structural changes that will encourage and support revitalized ministries, *The Holy and the Hybrid* should be on every pastor's, priest's, and lay minister's digital or old-school wooden desktop."

—Elizabeth Drescher, adjunct associate professor of religious studies, Santa Clara University; author of *Choosing Our Religion: The Spiritual Lives of America's Nones*

"*The Holy and the Hybrid* is a book every pastor and church leader needs to read. It invites us to reflect on the ways we were all thrown into the digital deep end during the pandemic, and most importantly, it offers a way forward for churches to develop sustainable hybrid ministries that will be essential for the future of the church."

—Jim Keat, digital minister, The Riverside Church

"In this timely book, Panzer skillfully identifies and interprets the moment we are in. With one foot in the church and one in the tech industry, he speaks with a hybridized authority that few of us can muster. *The Holy and the Hybrid* offers a feast of insights that will be beneficial to a wide range of church leaders navigating monumental cultural changes."

—Michael J. Chan, executive director for Faith and Learning, Concordia College, Moorhead, MN

"Part memoir, part manual, this readable book will help readers make sense of their own journeys into hybrid ministry—the places where the physical and the digital offer both old and new ways of doing ministry. Panzer is both committed to digital ministry and aware of its limits, which makes this book an honest and helpful guide for readers reflecting on how God is calling them to design the next chapter of ministry in their own settings."

—Dave Daubert, pastor, Zion Lutheran Church, Elgin, IL; lead consultant, Day 8 Strategies; and co-author of *Becoming a Hybrid Church*

"The coronavirus pandemic required us all to examine our way of life. What was essential? What could be modified? While we all scrambled with that in some way, churches and ministry organizations had the challenge of sharing the gospel and cultivating faithful community when most of the traditional communal practices of church were considered unsafe. In *The Holy and the Hybrid*, Ryan Panzer analyzes the emotions that came with the pandemic but also helps us learn and grow from the ways in which we had to adjust. Covid-19 forced us to examine the 'that's the way we've always done it' mentality in our churches and to look at how technology and digital practices can help our churches in their mission of sharing the gospel and cultivating faithful community. This book is not a 'how to do' but a 'how to think about' our ministry, allowing the logistics of tech-enhanced ministry to meet the culture and context of each congregation. *The Holy and the Hybrid* is a roadmap, or perhaps a GPS, pointing us to where the church can go in this next era of our ministry lives together."

—Ross Murray, deacon, Evangelical Lutheran Church in America; vice president, GLAAD Media Institute; founding director, The Naming Project; producer, *Yass, Jesus!* podcast; and author of *Made, Known, Loved: Developing LGBTQ-Inclusive Youth Ministry*

"Panzer reminds those of us who advocate for hybrid ministry what can be lost if we invest only in digital communities, and he challenges people who want to remove all cameras from church to consider what can be gained by offering everyone a front-row seat. If you are discerning to what extent digital ministry might, or might not, be a part of your congregation's future, this book won't provide easy answers. It will help you reflect on how your theological beliefs, understanding of community, and willingness to engage ethical uncertainty are important components of how, or if, you embrace a hybrid approach to ministry."

—Stacy Williams-Duncan, founder and CEO, Learning Forte

"Ryan Panzer is one of the most accessible and thoughtful Christians writing about digital tech in ministry today. Following upon his excellent first book, *Grace and Gigabytes*, he offers a resource-rich path through the uncertain spaces we are navigating as we move into the next chapters of church in and beyond a pandemic. He goes straight to the heart of the challenges when he writes, 'Digital Reformation is not a specific response to an event, but an effort to achieve a level of inclusivity that will benefit the church well after the worst of the pandemic has passed.'"

—Mary E. Hess, professor of educational leadership;
chair, leadership division, Luther Seminary

"Ryan Panzer is one for such a time as this, discipled in the theology and traditions of the church, yet also immersed in twenty-first-century tech culture. From this unique position, he offers a bold path forward for pastors and church leaders weary from the struggles of the Covid-19 pandemic, yet still faithfully seeking wisdom and direction to navigate the road ahead for their churches."

—Loren Richmond, pastor, podcaster, and social entrepreneur

"With a wealth of wisdom and experience in both the church and the tech industry, Panzer is exactly the voice we need to guide us into the Digital Reformation. His first book, *Grace and Gigabytes*, laid the conceptual foundation for the church's understanding of its place in our tech-shaped culture. *The Holy and the Hybrid* takes us deeper, asking what it means to be the church both online and offline. This book shines a light into the unseeable future, offering church leaders hope and instilling confidence that God is with us as we step into the hybrid adventure that awaits us."

—Jimmy Bero, youth pastor, Blackhawk Church, Madison, WI

"This is not another book on how to improve your church livestream or a quick-fix guide to building social media numbers. Panzer's invitation in *The Holy and the Hybrid* isn't even primarily about technology. He has written a winsome, clear-eyed, and hopeful invitation to the church to meet people wherever they are right now with the good news of Jesus. I'm deeply grateful for his thoughtful work and the way he continually points to the 'why' behind hybrid ministry."

—Eric Holmer, director of media,
Good Shepherd Lutheran Church, Madison, WI

THE HOLY AND THE HYBRID

THE
HOLY
AND THE
HYBRID

NAVIGATING THE CHURCH'S
DIGITAL REFORMATION

RYAN M. PANZER

Fortress Press
Minneapolis

THE HOLY AND THE HYBRID
Navigating the Church's Digital Reformation

Copyright © 2022 Fortress Press, an imprint of 1517 Media. All rights reserved.
Except for brief quotations in critical articles and reviews, no part of this book
may be reproduced in any manner without prior written permission from the
publisher. Email copyright@1517.media or write to Permissions, Fortress Press,
Box 1209, Minneapolis, MN 55440-1209.

Scripture quotations, unless otherwise noted, are from the New Revised Standard
Version Bible © 1989 Division of Christian Education of the National Council of
the Churches of Christ in the United States of America. Used by permission.

Scripture quotations marked (NIV) are taken from the Holy Bible, New
International Version®, NIV®. Copyright © 1973, 1978, 1984, 2011 by
Biblica, Inc.™ Used by permission of Zondervan. All rights reserved worldwide.
www.zondervan.com The "NIV" and "New International Version" are
trademarks registered in the United States Patent and Trademark Office by
Biblica, Inc.™

Cover design and illustration: Brad Norr Design

Print ISBN: 978-1-5064-8191-3
eBook ISBN: 978-1-5064-8192-0

For my son, Thomas.
May you always know the joy that comes with
deep connection and uplifting community.

The gifts he gave were that some would be apostles, some prophets, some evangelists, some pastors and teachers, *to equip the saints for the work of ministry*, for building up the body of Christ, until all of us come to the unity of the faith and of the knowledge of the Son of God, to maturity, to the measure of the full stature of Christ.

—Ephesians 4:11–13 (emphasis mine)

Contents

Preface

When I became interested in the topic of technology in the church, it seemed at times like a fringe or even futuristic topic. Some seminary courses, including those taught by Mary Hess at Luther Seminary, addressed the question of what it means to be church in a digital age. A few books, including *Click-2Save* by Keith Anderson and Elizabeth Drescher, offered insights for church leaders on social media and content creation. But the conversation on technology always seemed to have an experimental edge to it, as if digital expressions of Christian community were perhaps peripheral to the idea of church, the unique work of specialists as opposed to a church-wide vocation.

I wrote *Grace and Gigabytes* within this context. Among my motivations for writing the book was to persuade church leaders to think critically about technology. I hoped that readers would come to think about digital technology not just as a ministry tactic, but also as a cultural force that influences the way we think, know, and believe.

I submitted the final manuscript for the book on Wednesday, February 12, 2020. When I pressed "send," I never could have imagined how the pandemic would push church leaders to reinvent Christian community just four and a half weeks later. I never could have recognized that the book would come to be less about persuading leaders to think about digital ministry and more about accompanying them on what Tod Bolsinger, the author of *Canoeing the Mountains*, describes as a process of "leading off the map in charted territory."[1]

As I spoke with church leaders throughout an extended time of physical distancing and digital-only forms of church community, I gradually recognized that digital ministry was here to stay. As vaccines rolled out and buildings started to reopen, church leaders were no longer asking whether to gather as church in digital spaces. Their questions started to ask how best to put digital and analog together. How might we become a hybrid ministry that blends the best of online and offline? How might we build seamless connections in physical space and cyberspace? These were the questions I sought to answer as I started writing *The Holy and the Hybrid*.

In this book, I seek to define hybrid ministry as a blend of digital and analog that invites individuals to follow Christ and equips communities for faithful discipleship. I argue that hybrid ministry is the method best suited to proclaim the gospel to a digital age. And I suggest that its implementation represents a change-management challenge of historical magnitude.

I wrote this book to help church leaders navigate what Elizabeth Drescher first described as the "Digital Reformation." In her book, "*Tweet If You Heart Jesus: Practicing Church in the Digital Reformation*" Drescher defines the Digital Reformation as:

"A revitalization of the Church driven by the often ad hoc spiritualities of ordinary believers as they integrate practices of access, connection, participation, creativity, and collaboration, encouraged by the widespread use of new digital social media into all aspects of daily life, including the life of faith."[2] (p. 4)

Building on Drescher's pioneering work, this book seeks to accompany church leaders in this vocation of revitalization. This book is the product of countless conversations with thoughtful church leaders and technology enthusiasts who continue to courageously convene conversations on the church's hybrid future. Thank you to Luther Seminary's Faith Lead team—especially Dawn Alitz, Katie Langston, Emily McQuillan, Lara Moll, and Ben McDonald Coltvet, who led the way in hosting so many crucial conversations on this topic. The Faith Lead platform created a digital laboratory for church leaders eager for new models and methods, and many of the insights I present in this book emerged through their classes and discussions. Thank you to Michael Chan, with whom I prototyped and tested many of the ideas set forth in this book.

Thank you to the pastors and church leaders who have been so important in my faith life: Dennis Ellisen, Cindy Meyer, Kurt Hoffman, Sue Sprowls, Dave Hendricks, Sarah Iverson, Chris Enstad, Sheryl Erickson, Joe Brosious, Dara Schuller-Hanson, and of course, the late Brent Christianson.

Thank you to The Gentlemen's Book Club: Jim, Pete, Ray, Tim, Luke, Matt, and Mike. Our conversations on *Grace and Gigabytes* first inspired me to think about writing another book!

Thank you to the team at Fortress Press, especially Beth Gaede, who so thoughtfully edited this book as well as *Grace and Gigabytes*.

Finally, thank you to my wife, Annie, for providing essential everyday encouragement. And thank you to my kids, Alice and Thomas, who so delightfully remind me of the boundless joy in our life together!

INTRODUCTION

I noticed the dawning of the Digital Reformation on the afternoon of Friday, March 13, 2020. That was the day when many schools closed their doors and Disney shut down its theme parks. That was when every business that has your contact information sent you a message saying, "We're all in this together," the afternoon that the United States declared a national state of emergency. It's often said that those of us who are old enough, myself included, remember exactly where we were when we heard the news about 9/11, that most of my parents' generation remembers the moment they learned about the assassination of President Kennedy on November 22, 1963. We will surely remember in equal detail the emergence of Covid-19 and likely the cancelations and ominous directives from that Friday afternoon.

Many churches shuttered their buildings shortly thereafter, shelving their 2020 Lenten sermon series and spring volunteer schedules, along with Sunday school lesson plans and church announcement lists for the coming Sunday. That was the day when many of us realized that Covid-19 would be a historic and devastating event. Though we couldn't possibly have known it at the time, that March afternoon initiated a reimagination of Christian community, changes of a magnitude seldom seen since the Reformation of the sixteenth century.

I'll always remember where I was and what I was doing when I first realized the severity of our situation. I drove with my wife and daughter on the afternoon of Friday, March 13, to my grandmother's funeral. As we drove, we listened to XM Radio, hearing the worsening news from NPR and CNN. When a UCLA psychiatrist, calling from her home office, provided a lengthy radio segment on mindful coping through a long-term crisis, I knew that the world had changed, that this was far worse than anything resembling the seasonal flu. As I glanced out the driver's side window, I wondered where all of the cars and trucks on the still-bustling interstate could be heading, knowing full well that automobile traffic in the coming days would be much lighter.

After a drive of several hours, dread and anxiety swirling through my mind, we arrived at my grandma's memorial service. The funeral, held in a compact, stately Episcopal church, took place in a small town in central Wisconsin. Upon arrival, it was immediately clear that the recently declared pandemic had begun to change plans and alter behaviors. While a few days before, we had expected packed pews and an overfilled church, fears of the virus kept most friends away. Anxious and uncertain, we attempted to disconnect from the concerning headlines. Close relatives gathered in the nearly empty sanctuary, bright spring sunshine streaming through stained glass windows, to celebrate a full and abundant life and to mourn the passing of my grandmother, someone whose faithful devotion to family, community, and church would remain with us always.

After hearing the announcements that closed most church buildings in the area, several of us asked the priest not to serve the Eucharist. He begrudgingly agreed while maintaining that his Communion chalices contained special "antiviral alloys." Having seen the emerging information on social distancing, we also decided against handshakes and hugs, the funeral director sharing the requests on signs made of loose-leaf paper. As I sat in that old, nearly empty Episcopal church, where I had attended worship with my grandparents on countless Christmas Eves and Easter mornings, I wondered when we would next sit in the pews of a church. Amid the disorientation that comes from personal grief and profound global uncertainty, I worried about when we would next partake in the Lord's Supper, when we would next share the peace with the customary handshake. I worried about whether church would ever return to normal.

While many congregations began navigating the Digital Reformation that Friday, they found themselves fully immersed by the end of the weekend. It was on the third Sunday of Lent when many church leaders streamed worship online for the first time. Pastors preached their sermons, written to be proclaimed in a sanctuary, using smartphone cameras and social media. Congregations accustomed to hearing the words of Scripture reverberating through cavernous sanctuaries and auditoriums listened as the story of Jesus's encounter with a Samaritan woman was shared through Facebook. The lectionary text on the crossing of societal boundaries was fitting for a morning when some church communities gathered for worship beyond the threshold of the sanctuary for the first time. The Communion elements of bread and wine remained in cupboards, where in some parishes, they remained for many months. Baptismal fonts, replenished weekly with water in many churches, became parched from evaporation.

"I never thought I'd see the church this empty on Sunday morning," a pastor friend in southeast Michigan shared at the start of his church community's worship, streamed that morning on Facebook Live. "We have the coronavirus in our community, and I truly don't know what to do." Fidgeting, his eyes darted away from the camera. "I hope we can be together again soon. But for now, here we are. We're still going to try to be the church."

His candid sentiment was widespread that morning. Many churches simply canceled their Sunday worship, treating that first Sunday of the pandemic as if it were another winter day with weather conditions poorly suited for driving. Some church leaders resisted, continuing to gather their communities in sanctuaries until local governments explicitly closed church buildings.

That morning from 10:30 to 11:15 a.m. was the first time I participated in a virtual worship service. While I had previously joined services on video conferencing sites or caught glimpses of sermons on Facebook Live, these experiences had been passing background noise for work, road trips, and even camping. I would hardly have considered these sincere expressions of worship, at least relative to the Sunday morning traditions to which I was accustomed. Some of my experiences with exclusively online worship had been inadvertent, the result of an errant tap of the thumb as I scrolled the morning news feed. So as I sat next to my family on my couch, wearing sweatpants, I recognized that I would need to adapt my faith traditions and practice for an indefinite duration. All my past efforts to integrate the work of the church with new technology had prepared me to think about using digital tools in a church that maintained a consistent physical presence within a given neighborhood. My past work had not prepared me to think about using technology for many—and certainly not all—aspects of Christian community. It had not prepared me personally to worship exclusively with an online community. As we logged on to Facebook and connected the video feed to our television, I told my wife that "it was time to watch church," as if the acts of praying, hearing the Scriptures, and listening to preaching were in some way equivalent to watching reruns of *The Simpsons* or *The Sopranos*.

That morning there were also the logistical questions of "watching" church from the couch, questions we asked that morning and continued to ask for some time. Did we sing along with the musicians, and if so, how loudly? Did we stand for the hymn of the day? What would we do when the laundry cycle finished with a bundle of wet clothing still in the wash? What would we do when our phones rang? How would we pass the peace, and most importantly, how would we stay connected to our church family?

Throughout my career, I had long been an advocate for technology in the church. I had argued for more investment, for more opportunities to connect virtually. For years, I had grumbled when a council or committee meeting required a commute when a conference call would have sufficed, when a Bible study or book discussion required another trip out of the home after a long day at the office. But on that Sunday morning, when technology was all we had, I found myself surrounded by far more questions than answers. I found myself feeling restless, frustrated, even isolated. Maybe it was the shaky camera footage or the patchy audio quality. Maybe it was the fatigue that came from an emotionally and spiritually draining week or the anguish that came from reading the disconcerting headlines in the Sunday edition of the *Wisconsin State Journal*. But by the time that Service of the Word concluded with the blessing and benediction, I felt anything but reassured—about the church's presence online or about my ability to find spiritual sustenance through an exclusively virtual church community.

Recognizing that I had spent too many hours that weekend connected to a screen, I decided to venture out for a bike ride. With some trepidation, I sanitized the handlebars on my bicycle (an unnecessary act that wasted Clorox wipes, soon to become a commodity more precious than silver or gold) and wrapped a thin fabric neck gaiter, once used for sun protection while hiking and kayaking, around my mouth and nose. Battling gusty March winds, I pedaled past the churches in my neighborhood. The parking lot of my home church, a Lutheran congregation on the west side of Madison, Wisconsin, sat empty. The line of departing minivans and family SUVs that should have stretched across the lot was nowhere to be seen. There was a quiet grimness on the roads that Sunday, as cars that would have been going to brunch remained in the garage, as coffee shops that would have served scores of post-church visitors sat empty. As I biked, I passed one church that had declined to close their doors, their blaze-yellow parking lot signage conspicuous against a stretch of asphalt with only a few automobiles. As I pedaled, I passed another congregation that had failed to get the word out regarding cancelation, its confused members mulling around the front doors.

I returned home in time to try to catch a webinar, hosted by digital-ministry thought leaders I had interviewed for my first book. The webinar, simply titled "How to Do Church Online," promised to explain the basics of Facebook, Zoom, and YouTube, of video and audio equipment, of adaptations to liturgy. On that Sunday, when we thought about what it meant to be or to do church online, we thought exclusively about worship, because it was the item atop faith leaders' to-do lists. We could not have imagined that worship wouldn't be all that would move online, that faith formation, fellowship, service, and all aspects of our life together would soon become virtual. All I could think of on that afternoon was what it would take for so many faith communities to suddenly move worship online. So having heard of the webinar on Twitter, I promptly signed up, sharing the details with several of my colleagues trying to make sense of how to do church online. And as a sure sign of how quickly our lives had changed, I was denied admission to the event. The call, hosted on Zoom, had rapidly reached its five-hundred-person limit, well before its start time.

That afternoon, I felt disoriented from the magnitude of imminent change, weighed down by the realization of losses to come, yet also inspired by what I had witnessed in the church. In just forty-eight hours, many pastors and faith leaders had, for the safety and well-being of their communities, canceled in-person worship, cobbled together a plan for one online service, and began to assemble the pieces of a sustainable approach to digital ministry. When I think back on that March weekend, I don't think about technical glitches and hiccups in production quality. I think about the agility that faith leaders demonstrated, the innovation that we practiced. I think about how committed we were to learning and to leading. As so many in our tech-shaped culture, myself at times included, spent that weekend "doom-scrolling" through worst-case-scenario posts on social media, the church met the moment with resilience and a commitment to following God's call through unprecedented uncertainty.

Still, there was so much we didn't know, so much we had no way of imagining that mid-March weekend. What we couldn't yet recognize at the time was how this rapid pivot from sanctuaries to streaming would be the first decisive step in a permanent reimagining of Christian community. We couldn't yet realize that a time of digital distribution would force us not just to move worship online but to reinvent every aspect of our life together. We couldn't yet see that our model of leading churches, of convening, uplifting, and sustaining Christian communities, would soon be completely upended. We couldn't imagine on that Sunday, when the newspapers spoke of little more than the surging pandemic, the significant change we were about to experience.

The questions raised on that Sunday morning indicated that the Digital Reformation is no discrete set of tasks defined by tidy checklists that can be completed through one-off installations or single-step integrations. The Digital Reformation is a process of discernment, of living into a new way of being church. It is a process of integrating the deep connections of the offline with the wide connectivity of the online. Streaming worship online, going to church online—these are merely first steps.

AN ONGOING BALANCE

The Digital Reformation accelerated when churches moved online due to the coronavirus's health risks. But the Digital Reformation was not and is not a story of a temporary, even if prolonged, transition to exclusively online church. Virtual worship and the digital forms of community we experienced during the early days of the pandemic were preliminary milestones on a transformation of Christian community, a transformation that will continue for years.

Those who worry that the future of church will be entirely digital should understand that Christian community will never be exclusively, or even primarily, virtual. There will be some exceptions, as in congregations that gather exclusively through social media or in virtual reality, models that are described further in chapter 2. Yet in an environment of content saturation and rampant digital distraction, even the best of these examples is difficult to manage and sustain. The Digital Reformation is not a movement toward churches without neighborhoods, worship without sanctuaries, or communities without face-to-face connections. Instead, the Digital Reformation is best understood as a gradual and continuous reimagining of what it means to be the church in the digital age—to align the shared mission of the church and the shared values of our tech-shaped culture, to strive toward the optimal balance of face-to-face community and virtual connection.

This reimagining comes with visible markers, including use of optimized technology and less ambivalence about virtual forms of community. Faith communities are becoming more fluent in deploying digital tools, using personalized technologies that facilitate faith formation, and working together through collaborative apps and resources. But these visible markers are insufficient in defining the contours of the Digital Reformation. This movement is about more than apps and streaming cameras, podcasts and playlists. At its core is the emergence of a new mindset. The Digital Reformation involves a commitment to reversing the widespread idea that authentic Christian community requires synchronous, physical gatherings. As we continue to gather face-to-face, the Digital Reformation needs leaders willing to accompany communities that live within a tech-shaped culture, where there are fewer and fewer distinctions between the online and the offline.

As with any major transition, some among us will resist the ongoing changes. Rather than exploring the necessary yet often invisible work of aligning Christian leadership to a tech-shaped culture, some will adopt a "set it and forget it" approach. Some leaders will complete the installation of new tech without continuously balancing virtual and physical community. They will implement, but they will not iterate. They will purchase new software and services but stop short of critical reflection on what it means to form a blended church community.

The long-term challenge of the Digital Reformation is to build a bridge between face-to-face community, once the definitive model of Christian community, and the virtual forms of togetherness that became our primary form of connection. The goal is to build communities to serve as the hands and feet of Christ simultaneously online and offline. This isn't the discrete task of a single moment but the complex calling of a new epoch in the Christian tradition. This isn't a tidy to-do list that will take weeks or months to complete but a vocation that will take years to live into.

AN EMERGENT REFORMATION

Past reformations have asked new questions about church doctrine, theology, and leadership, calling into question the content and cadence of communal life, always seeking to uplift and edify. Similarly, in this moment, we call into question the shape and structure of our communal life: how, when, and where we gather. As we discern how our faith communities might become a hybrid of the online and the offline, we must adopt the mindset not of a technologist or a media professional but of a church reformer, of one who is remaking and remolding the church, responding with agility to our tech-shaped culture—always so that more might come to know Christ and collaborate in God's global mission.

This transformation in the location of Christian community shares two parallels with the Protestant Reformation of sixteenth- and seventeenth-century Europe. First, our present transformation and the Protestant Reformation were catalyzed by technological change. In 1517, Gutenberg's invention of a movable type printing press made it possible to widely circulate the writings of Martin Luther, expanding the church's imagination about how to connect with a more literate and individuated culture. Today, the proliferation of mobile, high-speed computing has made it possible to find virtual forms of church community, expanding our imagination about what it means to do ministry with a more connected and collaborative culture.

The second parallel is open-endedness. Even if triggered by a specific event, the implications of a reformation can take considerable time to discover. A reformation is a process of reimagining and reworking, discussion and debate, improvisation and iteration. These processes require the careful navigation of necessary changes and time-honored traditions. In sixteenth- and seventeenth-century Europe, an increasingly literate society became more engaged in faith practices through translated, accessible Scripture. In our Digital Reformation, an increasingly wired society may become more connected to faith practices and more dedicated to exploring the contours of the life of faith as Christian community becomes more accessible.

In my 2020 book, *Grace and Gigabytes: Being Church in a Tech-Shaped Culture*, I identify why the digital age necessitates innovation and reinvention from church leaders. I also describe how the culture of our digital age has come to prioritize learning through questions, connecting seamlessly offline and online, engaging in collaborative service, and expressing personal creativity. The book traces how these shared cultural values mutually reinforced core design principles of our most popular technologies: questions edified through search engines, new forms of connection strengthened through messaging tools, collaboration facilitated through apps like Google Docs, and creativity supported by platforms like Instagram and YouTube. While our most ubiquitous technologies influence how we think, learn, and believe, I contend in the book that being the church in the digital age is not about using technology. Rather, being a church in this era is about aligning with these values, embracing the definitive aspects of tech-shaped culture as we continue to proclaim the Word and administer the sacraments. I then describe how all faith communities—no-tech, low-tech, and high-tech—could connect with these values for the sake of a greater alignment with this cultural moment. I remain committed to these core arguments. The more church leaders embrace questions, connection, collaboration, and creativity, the more missional our faith communities can become and the more effectively we can equip communities for lives of faithful service. Church will be at its best when we begin our conversations on technology not with apps or IT infrastructure but with culture. This approach can benefit all Christian communities, strengthening their capacity to share the gospel in this digital age.

As I spoke to groups of faith leaders in the year after *Grace and Gigabytes* was published, however, I realized that these values are useful starting points that require further exploration. I heard questions about the best way to prioritize these cultural values and the best strategies for putting the framework into practice. I heard concerns about what these values mean for low-tech or even no-tech congregations and how these values can be practiced in change-averse communities. I also heard conversations that started with these cultural values but drifted into the minutiae of information technology, the mundane and often trivial side of tech that alienates those who consider themselves "nontechie." As we continue to move further from what we once knew as "normal" in our churches, church leaders will likely encounter three challenges to implementing the ideas within *Grace and Gigabytes*.

First, although congregations recognize the four cultural values, they are unclear about which one to engage first. These are questions of initiation, or ignition, and are often asked by church communities that are eager to implement some of the ideas in the book. A second challenge is skeptical communities, those who fear a continued digitization of church. These are questions of change and transition management, typically arising in church communities that are eager to unplug computers, cameras, and microphones and gather in person as soon as possible. Third, many congregations seem content to bypass the culture conversation altogether, jumping into decisions about hardware and software without considering how to align with questions, collaboration, connection, and creativity.

As I've reflected on these questions of initiation, transition management, and implementation, I have come to recognize that these four digital-age values necessitate a process of implementation and iteration. If these ideas are to find their way into the workings of an innovative church, they need to be examined in light of a prepandemic way of doing church that prioritizes in-person community as well as a pandemic model of doing church that depended on digital distribution. Being the church in a tech-shaped culture will always involve questions, connection, collaboration, and creativity. But the early days of the pandemic changed my understanding of how we ought to live into these values, a perspective I explore in this book.

Hybrid ministry brings together online practices of invitation and offline practices of equipping-online, inviting both members and the broader community to come and follow Christ; offline, preparing members and the broader community alike to serve the neighbor. To be clear, inviting in digital spaces is no simple task. It is far more involved than creating a digital event invitation. To *invite* in the context of the Digital Reformation is to step into the web and boldly welcome people to engage in a congregation's mission and ministry. This profoundly important work emerges from the digital-age values of questions and connections. Through our inviting presence in digital spaces, we provide opportunities for people to connect in new ways and to question what it would mean to follow Christ in the digital age.

A church that *equips* in offline, or analog, spaces creates encounters where community members discover what it means to love one another. This work reflects the digital-age values of collaboration and creativity. Through our equipping face-to-face practices, we discern how to serve one another in light of the narratives of Scripture and our personal experience. This equipping emerges from and is undergirded by the grace of God first encountered through worship, through Word and sacrament.

If the Digital Reformation encompasses a broad movement within the church toward a greater alignment with our tech-shaped culture, then hybrid ministry is our method. This method builds on the rich traditions of prepandemic, in-person faith community and affirms the strengths of digital technologies, which enable us to gather a more connected cloud of witnesses. It minimizes the exclusivity of the in-person church, which precludes the involvement of those who cannot be physically present due to distance and transportation limitations, work or family commitments, or health situations. It also minimizes the distress and disruptions experienced in exclusively virtual forms of church—the tendency to passively watch a screen, the need to acquire hardware and software, and the learning curve for effectively using digital technology. Whether no-tech, low-tech, or high-tech, we must commit to hybrid forms of church to build a bridge between the offline and the online and to align with the cultural values first described in *Grace and Gigabytes*.

WHY NOW?

At the end of that day—Sunday, March 15, 2020—I looked back on all that had changed in just one week. The previous weekend had been a full one at my church. In a jam-packed church building, I had ladled chili from slow cookers to dozens of hungry diners as part of the congregation's annual chili cook-off. I had preached a sermon to a sanctuary full of parishioners, many of whom sat elbow to elbow, and shared a children's sermon with dozens of kids, many of them freely climbing around the altar railing. The sermon series the congregation had selected that Lent was titled "A Spiritual Reboot." Little did I know, standing in the pulpit that Sunday morning, that the idea of a reboot—a momentary, instantaneous restart—would seem so unsubstantial, so minuscule given the grand scale of what was about to take place.

Late that Sunday night, I reclined in my favorite chair, taking a moment to scroll through my news feeds. It was the first time I had been online since early Friday, and it was clear the world had changed. Set amid the worst-case scenario posts on projected case numbers and economic fallout, I managed to find a bit of subtle levity in my church circles. It was, after all, still Lent. Just three weeks had passed since Ash Wednesday. "This year for Lent, I'm giving up literally everything," a post from an Episcopal friend exclaimed. "Well, we now know that this is the 'Lentiest' Lent of all Lents," a Lutheran pastor shared a few days later.

But in a way, it's fitting that the great disruptions of the pandemic emerged during Lent. It is, after all, a liturgical season of turning around, of repenting, of intentionally facing a different direction, of choosing a different alignment. From the imposition of ashes on Ash Wednesdays to the personal disciplines many of us take up for forty days, Lent is a time to pivot away from that which holds us back in our walk with Christ as we attempt to travel another route.

Embracing the Digital Reformation by living into hybrid ministry will be a continuous process of turning. We'll have to turn away from ways of being the church that don't hold up to the realities of a relentlessly changing culture. We'll be required to turn away from models of Christian community that don't invite, that fail to equip, that only feign collaboration. And we'll have to let go of the idea that one-time resets and quick reboots can address the magnitude of cultural transition that the church must grapple with.

The Digital Reformation isn't just a single season of turning, however. It is a years-long embrace of continuous change. We take up this work not for the sake of relevance or trendiness but for the sake of the gospel, not to promote institutional longevity but to form disciples. We start on this road not to boost attendance nor improve finances, not to share success stories nor to describe ourselves as a "growing" church. We start on this road because it is the only path that can lead our culture to a transforming experience of the grace of God. This is the sacred vocation to which all church leaders—lay and ordained, adult and youth, staff and member, neighbor and visitor—are called.

THE LAST COFFEE HOUR

ANALOG CHURCH, DISRUPTED

It wasn't the building that I missed the most. It wasn't the sound of organ music echoing through the sanctuary. It wasn't preaching from a pulpit, children's sermons at the altar railing, or the cool touch of the offering plates passed across the rows.

What I missed the most on Sunday, March 15, 2020, were the doughnuts. And I don't mean eating the doughnuts, which were often stale, rather flavorless, and not worth the numbers they added to my jeans size. I mean the conversations that surrounded the doughnuts, the pleasant chatter that filled the lobby every Sunday morning at approximately 11:02 a.m. I missed the small talk with close friends, especially the cross-generational friends who were in many cases even older than my grandparents. I missed the banter with the coffee hosts, the repeatable yet irrepressible jokes about the volunteer baristas doing the real "Lord's work."

I missed the sign-up sheets for book discussions and donation boxes for homeless ministries, the volunteer sign-up tables, and the calendar displays, all consistently busy locations amid the caffeinated conversation hour. I missed shaking hands with visitors my age, visitors I hoped would come again yet who were statistically unlikely to return. I missed walking out the side door, a refilled cup of coffee in my hands and doughnut crumbs on my shirt, the sun glinting off the snowbanks. When I look back to that first Sunday of church online, I missed the moments of connection—simple, sometimes awkward, yet ever-uplifting moments where we shared our stories and felt heard.

Those conversations over coffee and doughnuts renewed our commitments to close friends, new acquaintances, and fellow members. The church we were prior to the Covid-19 pandemic was a place of life-giving encounters, a place where we went to discover and live into the idea that we are all human beings looking for connection and purpose. It was a place where we belonged. That sense of togetherness helped us see that our acts of faithful service for the good of the neighbor made a real difference to them.

I also realized on March 15, 2020, as I recognize today, that not every connection is friendly, fulfilling, and faith-filled. Churches are places for imperfect people, simultaneously saint and sinner, keen to bring their full selves but not always their best selves to church. Anyone who has ever preached a sermon and been subjected to immediate postservice feedback knows that congregants can pivot from friendly to fractious, from constructive to critical.

Yet when I think about the disagreements over politics and polity and the nit-picking over the smallest changes to worship styles or liturgy, I am reminded that face-to-face connections in the church form us for service to a real world, an actual place of friendship and resentment, agreement and discord. I am reminded that the bonds of church membership and participation—the good and the bad of it all—rapidly form us for a relational depth that no social media page or group chat could offer.

We always left by 11:15, or by 11:30 if Annie and I were serving our quarterly coffee host assignment. Coffee and doughnuts lasted no more than thirteen minutes for me. Yet those minutes filled up my prayer lists and my Christmas card list. Those brief moments each Sunday established deep, cross-generational trust with people I hardly knew, with people I often disagreed with, and with people for whom I would do anything. At 11:15 a.m. on March 15, 2020, we had no place from which to depart, nobody to wave to, no parking lot to cross, no car to start. We had watched an online service with preaching and prayer, Scripture and singing, and plenty of announcements about what would become the church's new normal. But we were missing our sense of connection with our church community. We were missing togetherness.

I wish I had known on Sunday, March 8, 2020, as I walked out of the last coffee hour, how much the world would change. I don't remember much about that specific morning, aside from the fact that I was preaching and that there had been some nervous chatter and anxious conversation about the virus's increasing spread within the United States. I do remember that we decided on fist bumps instead of handshakes for the passing of the peace, that someone had placed a large jug of hand sanitizer next to the doughnuts, and that the coffee-hour hosts were filling up paper cups instead of letting each congregant fill their own mugs. I wish I would have known on that last Sunday of "ordinary time" how much I would miss these connections. I wish I would have paused to take it all in and express some gratitude and appreciation for the togetherness that was so foundational to the church we were.

CONNECTION IN THE ANALOG CHURCH

Before the pandemic, two markers of the church stood out to me as a thirtysomething with an interest in technology. The first marker was its analog quality. Before the pandemic, walking into most church buildings felt like a trip through a time machine. While some churches had computers and Wi-Fi connections, church staff and lay leaders typically viewed the web as a communications tool rather than a mission field or a ministry site. Cell phones were often viewed more as nuisances than as tools for inviting or equipping, their apps and notifications a source of distraction and encumberment.

As a former camp counselor and youth ministry worker, I now recognize that I spent far too much time and energy trying to keep kids unplugged from technology for a Sunday morning, a Wednesday evening, or a week at camp. I mastered an extensive set of techniques for removing digital distractions, from "Cell Phone Jails" to voluntary device drop boxes. At the time, I believed it was worth my time to constantly ask kids to disconnect from screens. I may have thought that it was more important to remove digital distractions than to talk to the youth about what it means to be a Christian in their busy world. I and many other church leaders were determined to pivot youths' energy and attention away from the digital, which we viewed as a source of interruption, and toward the analog, which we assumed to be the authentic location of Christian community. I now wish that instead of blocking access to devices, we had found ways to convene Christian community and conversation online. While moments of digital Sabbath are always important to the life of faith, I should have sought not just to eliminate tech usage in the church but to integrate it into the life of the community.

Yes, the analog, nondigital church has some clear limitations, including difficulty connecting with the surrounding community. On the other hand, it also provides a buffer from the demands of the outside world. The analog church offers a level of spiritual insulation that strengthens the connections that develop through the church. In the prepandemic church, I always appreciated the opportunity to temporarily unplug from email, communication apps, and social media. Without social pressures to constantly check in with work or log on to my ever-increasing array of messaging applications, I saw the congregation as a place where I could be fully present.

The other marker of the analog church is its ties to a fixed time and location. Prior to the pandemic, everything about the church took place at specific times and, most importantly, in specific places. Particularly in urban mainline Protestant congregations, some of which occupy historic downtown buildings, institutional and family loyalty inspires congregants to commute from the suburbs or exurbs, sometimes great distances, to worship together.

Some aspects of a fixed locale and synchronous practice are problematic, though. For example, many churchgoers pay little attention to a congregation's mission and ministry outside the church walls. It's true that most churchgoers travel less than ten minutes to arrive at a church building.[1] But increasingly, churches are destinations for members traveling past the surrounding neighborhood—one where, outside of the building, they have few if any meaningful connections. Facilities also require a major financial investment. Recent studies of church finances have revealed that as much as twenty-five cents of every dollar donated to the church goes toward facility costs and upkeep.[2] Having volunteered with fundraising and other campaigns for several different churches and church-affiliated ministries, I've seen how the costs of physical structures captivate both our balance sheets and our imagination of what ministry could and should be.

Still, there are advantages to fixed locations. In addition to the practical benefits of shelter and safety, buildings provide a consistent physical presence in a neighborhood that creates a tangible symbol of communal life, which can in turn inspire a sense of shared ownership or stewardship. Having a building binds the abstract concepts of community and discipleship to the congregation's identity and commitments. More concretely, the site provides a consistent setting for acts of service and volunteerism, for putting one's faith in action for the good of the neighbor. I have at times criticized church leaders' tendencies to invest too many resources and too much energy in facilities, a commitment I believe can isolate Christian communities from their surrounding neighborhoods while inhibiting innovation in digital spaces. Nevertheless, it is difficult to fathom how faith communities would be as efficient or as effective in equipping members and neighbors for lives of faithful service without investing in local settings for hearing and telling one another's stories.

How Connections Form Us

The church's nondigital, localized, and synchronous qualities contribute to a shared sense of togetherness. But these connections are not the exclusive domain of faith communities. Coffee shops and happy hours create connection and togetherness, as do book clubs and shopping malls. What is distinctive about togetherness in the church is not that it exists but that it catalyzes concrete acts of service at a pace unmatched in other institutions. Togetherness in a faith community is unique because the congregation provides opportunities to enact shared spiritual values and faith commitments, to make a difference in a community. Sociologists have thoroughly chronicled how participating in a faith-based community significantly increases the likelihood that people will be civically engaged and active in social and political causes and that they will freely volunteer in the community.[3]

Social capital is an abstract concept that may not be familiar outside of academic circles, but it is important for understanding the strengths of the church we were. Social capital refers to a web of relationships that can be activated in working together toward a common purpose.[4] In a religious context, social capital refers to "social resources available to individuals and groups through their social connections within a religious community."[5] As political scientists Pippa Norris and Ronald Inglehart concluded in their study "Religious Organizations and Social Capital," "Mainline Protestant churches play a vital role in drawing together diverse groups of Americans within local communities, encouraging face-to-face contact, social ties and organizational networks that, in turn, generate interpersonal trust and collaboration over public affairs.

The theory suggests that people who pray together often also stay together to work on local matters, thereby strengthening communities."[6] When we belong to a church community, we serve more, we speak up more, and we listen more. There's even evidence that our physical health improves![7]

Sociologist Robert Putnam has studied the many ways that active participation with a faith community inclines us toward generosity and equips us for service. His book *American Grace: How Religion Divides and Unites Us* details how religious individuals are more inclined to be generous, to volunteer in secular and religious causes, to advocate for social change, and to exhibit higher levels of social trust.[8] According to Putnam's research, frequent churchgoers are even more likely to donate blood.[9] Putnam's findings appear to indicate that something about involvement within a church community activates prosocial tendencies.

Many of these altruistic behaviors correlate not just with membership or belief but with the frequency of attendance at religious services. Putnam reports that those who attend church services weekly, or even occasionally, are significantly more likely to be trusting and generous than those who never attend worship.[10] This finding seems to suggest that it's not just claiming Christian identity but participating in a network of Christian social connections that forms individuals for altruism. In other words, when we show up and connect with others, we develop a service-oriented mindset. It is participation within the community, and not just affiliation, that inspires an individual toward service and generosity.

As a sociologist, Putnam is quick to remind his readers that correlation does not imply causation and that despite the statistical rigor of his analysis, there is always a chance that the high levels of altruism and generosity within faith communities may simply be a product of altruistic individuals naturally gravitating toward church membership. In fact, he contends, this tendency toward altruism is not the result of our beliefs or personal practices but instead a direct result of the connections created within congregations. As Putnam concludes, "Theology and piety have very little to do with this religious edge in neighborliness and happiness. Instead, it is religion's network of morally freighted personal connections, coupled with an inclination towards altruism, that explains both the good neighborliness and the life satisfaction of religious Americans."[11]

What's remarkable is that this correlation is catalyzed by relatively small investments of time. In 2014, only one in three members of the Evangelical Lutheran Church in America (ELCA), the largest Lutheran denomination in the United States (also the denomination in which I was raised), attended worship services on a weekly basis.[12] One out of three members attend several times throughout the year, and one out of three never attend. This means that if you select a member of the ELCA, or any Christian denomination at random, and ask how much time they spend at church or with their church in a given week, more likely than not, their answer would be less than one hour. In fact, on average, Americans spend only 8.4 minutes per day on religious or spiritual activities. By contrast, the average American watches 168 minutes of television each day.[13] Even though we don't spend many hours at church or with religious activities, the social capital correlations remain. In the fleeting moments one might spend at church, connections form, which in turn form the individual for service and altruism. Why are churches so efficient, then,

27

at equipping for acts of service with comparatively few time resources?

From Connections to Service

The theological foundation of the church is the grace of God encountered first through Word and sacrament. Service to the neighbor is our response to God's redeeming action; it turns us outward to love and serve the neighbor. As church leaders, our primary vocation is to ensure consistent access to Word and sacrament. While equipping individuals for service may not itself be the theological foundation of Christian community, nevertheless, the ability of churches to equip individuals for service is a distinctive aspect of congregational life. According to a 2016 Pew study, access to service opportunities is among the top factors contributing to one's choice of a faith community.[14]

Churches are effective at equipping for service for many reasons, some of them having to do with traditional aspects of Christian life together. The call to service is in the DNA of the church community. When gathering on Sunday mornings, we see and hear exhortations to care for the neighbor. We hear sermons that articulate how the Scriptures set us free for good works toward our neighbor. We see sign-up sheets and bulletin boards describing how we might get involved. If we come back to the building during the week, we participate in concrete acts of service: sorting donations for the clothes closet, preparing food for a community Thanksgiving meal, or making Christmas decorations for the local nursing home.

Even as America's religious landscape secularizes and diversifies, and even as churches evolve from an analog model, we can still expect faith communities to be accelerators of social capital, equipping individuals to live out the teachings of their faith. Preaching, proclamation, and spiritual practices provide a framework that inspires us to service, but it is still through our connections that we receive concrete and specific opportunities to practice our faith. The synchronous, in-person church, the only experience most of us knew prior to March 2020, was particularly competent at forming and sustaining weak ties, a type of connection that can convert ideas into action.

We might define a weak tie as a connection with a person whose primary social, professional, and religious circles occasionally intersect with our own. These acquaintances or casual connections occur within a nonfamilial network, such as membership within the same church. Weak ties serve as a "social lubricant" that facilitates the exchange of ideas and the sharing of resources, along with mutually uplifting contributions.[15] By contrast, a strong tie is a deep friendship or significant familial bond. When I think about my connections, my strong ties are the individuals on my Christmas card list, the friends and family who attended my wedding. I consider my relationships with most of the people I work, attend church, and serve with to be weak ties. The localized church easily creates networks of weak ties, which inspire us to love and serve the neighbor.

Some might suggest that it is diminishing or disrespectful to categorize a relationship, especially a relationship formed in Christian community, as a weak tie. The word *weak* connotes insignificance, implying that weak ties are not important. This might be why we don't use it much in church circles. Robert Putnam, author of *Bowling Alone*, argues, however, that weak ties create bridges between individuals, sustaining a norm of "generalized reciprocity."[16] For Putnam and other researchers of social capital, the "weakness" of these ties is their great strength. According to his surveys, our acquaintances and casual friends are the primary reasons we remain in a faith community and are even more important than the quality and style of worship and music.[17] Weak ties open the door to collaboration and service because they provide abundant opportunities through which to practice our faith. They both alert us to needs and connect us to the settings where our service will benefit others. They also often provide tools and resources needed for enacting one's faith.

In addition, sociologists point out the remarkable resiliency of weak ties. They have a unique ability to remain dormant for an extended duration, only to immediately activate in times of need. When we need help, when we need a problem solved, we will likely find a solution from a dormant tie, from someone we haven't spoken with in months or even years. And our dormant ties tend to readily agree to help, even if it's been years since we last spoke.

A recent experience illustrates the relationship between weak ties and good works. A few years ago, I was visiting a rural Wisconsin congregation. During the announcements after the sermon, the priest shared that one of the elderly members of the parish, who was not a regular churchgoer, had lost their husband and needed help moving into a smaller home. Without family in the area, the woman had no one else to turn to. A visitor raised his hand and volunteered the use of his pickup truck. Another congregation member offered to help move furniture. The priest offered to pack boxes. The voices rose from across the pews as people with weak ties in the community committed to serving their neighbor that very afternoon.

Beginning on Sunday, March 15, 2020, and every subsequent Sunday until the reopening of our sanctuary, it wasn't the people with whom I had strong ties that I missed seeing. For the most part, I stayed in contact with that handful of people in my church through texting, Facebook Messenger, and the occasional video call. What I now know I was missing were the weak ties, the casual acquaintances I would greet during the passing of the peace and converse with over coffee and doughnuts. I missed the connections with whom I would largely lose contact Monday through Saturday but whom I would inevitably see again at worship, where together, we could respond to the liturgy's work of sending the community to shoulder one another's burdens.

Exclusively or predominantly online forms of church community might involve a lot of connections. They might reach a lot of people who are eager to serve. They likely include familiar exhortations and attempts at equipping for service, calling us to respond to the divine calling we hear when we worship together in person. What online forms of church tend to lack are the mundane moments that facilitate encounters, the occasions when connections are formed, stories are shared, and bridges are built. A church that is digitized, which might involve little more than passive viewership and scrolling, is limited in its ability to establish connections that lead to service. This is the reason we cannot relinquish face-to-face forms of Christian community in a late-pandemic or postpandemic church. Amid all of the changes in the church's Digital Reformation, we must find a way to maintain connections and networks.

WHY CHURCHES NEED DIGITAL COMMUNITY

Some readers will inevitably ask, If face-to-face faith communities are so effective at creating social capital, and thus equipping members for lives of faithful service, why do anything differently? With the strengths of in-person Christianity well established in both academic research and the anecdotal experience of countless church leaders, why is the Digital Reformation worth navigating?

To answer this question, we have to consider the importance of accompaniment in the missional church. Members of a localized church are limited in their ability to walk alongside communities in a digital and secular age. We thus seek to augment the face-to-face faith community through digital experiences of church so we can accompany our neighbor, hearing and attending to their experiences in the virtual spaces where they share stories.

Some will look at recent well-documented declines in church attendance and membership as evidence that the analog church is not effectively extending the broadest possible invitation to an encounter with God's grace, as experienced within the institutional church. The size of America's churchgoing population shrank by thirteen percentage points from 2007 through 2019, dropping from 78 percent to 65 percent of American adults.[18] Similarly, in that same span, the size of America's religiously unaffiliated population increased by nine percentage points, from 17 percent to 26 percent.[19] Others will point to declining donations as a clear sign of the limits of face-to-face faith communities. The percentage of Americans who donated to a religious charity has fallen at a similar rate as religious affiliation, with a 12 percent decline from 2005, when 64 percent of American adults donated to a church or church charity, to 2017, when the figure was 52 percent.[20]

Yet while these indicators are interesting, they are merely signs, not root causes, of a deeper cultural shift. They are only symptoms of a broader challenge confronting the digital age church. And if church leaders want to preserve the proclamation of the church within the digital age, they would do well to focus their efforts on the root causes of these downward trends.

We could study the effect of secularization on church membership or lament about families prioritizing other activities over worship attendance. But maybe our energy is best directed toward a manageable opportunity: how might we encounter people where they are? The localized character of the prepandemic church has inhibited our presence in digital spaces. We can't extend a broad invitation to collaborate in God's work, the work of the church, if we don't put ourselves in contexts where communities congregate—namely, the web.

Church social media and website usage increased steadily prior to 2020, although estimates vary on church engagement in digital spaces. Some surveys have identified that approximately eight out of ten churches used websites and social media prior to the pandemic.[21] Other studies have identified a number closer to five out of ten.[22] Many of these surveys poll churches in a specific denomination, and the surveys that draw more responses from evangelical respondents tend to report higher levels of digital media usage, consistent with the tendency of evangelical churches to be early adopters of emerging technology.

While it's difficult to pinpoint the extent of digital media usage, we can make some observations about the quality of church presence in digital spaces. In the analog church, most of the digital tactics were developed to promote synchronous, in-person experiences. Church social media postings resembled a calendar or bulletin boards. They shared dates, times, and locations of in-person events but did not convene conversations, establish relationships, or extend an invitation to involvement or service. Social media were deployed as an extension of church communications, akin to a weekly newsletter or a worship bulletin. Social media tasks were typically assigned to the same individual responsible for curating the calendar and sending out congregational mailings.

In the analog church, the information we broadcasted through the web included dates and times, addresses and staff contacts, all attempting to convince community members to show up at a particular time and location. As church leaders, we used the web to announce that ministry was taking place somewhere else. We viewed the internet as a mechanism for sharing that the life of the church was happening and that one could participate, if only one were willing to sign off the web and sign up for something happening elsewhere. Seldom did we use the web for dialogue and deep connection.

If you want to see the extent to which churches used digital tools prepandemic simply for broadcasting, announcing, and scheduling, look at their social media posts prior to March 2020. I recently looked back at the Facebook page from a church I occasionally visited while growing up in northern Wisconsin. In February 2020, they posted to Facebook exactly two times. One post shared a PDF of the church newsletter; the other listed the worship start time for Ash Wednesday. Typical of most churches, these posts were intended to convince web users to go somewhere else, to engage with the exclusively offline life of a faith community.

Still, churches are getting better at using the web to build relationships and conversation. We're learning quickly. In February 2021, eleven months after the start of the pandemic, that same church posted to social media nearly twenty times. Their posts included collaborative conversations: polls, questions, devotional discussions, and prompts for sermon reflections. Several members of the community, both rostered leaders and church attendees, contributed content, sharing, listening to, and commenting on stories and perspectives from the now digitally distributed faith community. There were graphics, quotes, memes, and prayers. There were attempts to listen to the community on how it felt to navigate month twelve of the pandemic. Changes in that church's Facebook page revealed that this community has developed hybrid ministry practices of accompanying and equipping. Similar improvements in other church digital media platforms show that we may in fact be closer to being the church we must become. In the church we must become, we will not just announce and inform. We will actually do ministry in digital spaces, inviting communities into lived experiences of collaborative ministry that happen both online and offline.

With the ongoing growth in digital technology usage throughout society, the church's consistent inviting and collaborative presence in digital environments will be particularly important. Tech-shaped culture was deeply invested in the web prior to March 2020. Then in the first months of the pandemic, Facebook saw a 27 percent increase in usage.[23] Netflix viewing rose by 16 percent. Zoom, which became a key platform for Christian worship and faith formation, saw its usage jump from ten million users in December 2019 to three hundred million users in April 2020—only four months. The pandemic elevated usage of digital tools, accelerating our movement into a culture that is deeply formed and shaped by technology. As these trends continue, we'll need to discover not just how to communicate on social media but how to connect and collaborate. We'll need to learn to be together and to serve together online. With the average American now spending over two hours per day on social media, we'll need to discover what it means to be invitational online, even as we remain committed to traditional forms of in-person connection that catalyze service and generosity.

But there's a second, more practical reason we must move beyond the exclusively analog church. The synchronous, building-based form of church was a "one size fits most" approach to faith community. Since most of our community was available on Sunday morning and reliably lived within a short trip of our building, in-person church was both practical and sustainable. But in the digital age, an analog form of church fits fewer people with each passing year. Sunday mornings are no longer insulated from the demands of the outside world. While we could and arguably should lament this trend as the encroachment of secularization on the sacred, we're unlikely to reverse the advance of the broader culture into Sunday morning. As of 2015, one in three of us work on Sunday mornings, while half of those who work more than one job are occupied on Sunday.[24]

If our work activities are not encroaching on Sunday morning, social activities and sports are. One in four kids plays basketball, hockey, or volleyball, youth sports that regularly schedule tournaments on weekends, including Sunday mornings.[25] These challenges are not new to church leaders, who have long seen kids leaving summer camp early for a Little League game, who have observed parents pulling their youth out of the confirmation retreat for a karate class. Even Sunday nights aren't safe from encroachments on time and energy. Seventy-six percent of us report feeling the "Sunday Scaries" or "Sunday Night Blues," a feeling of anticipatory stress that leads to the constant checking of email, messages, and calendars in an often-futile attempt to alleviate the pressures of the coming workday.[26]

Organizers of work, sports, and social activities once avoided scheduling events on Sunday mornings. Today, these demands are unrelenting. And if we find ourselves with a "free" Sunday, many of us now view it as an occasion to accomplish the items on our to-do lists that we couldn't complete earlier in the week. This trend has made it difficult for churches to continue to operate with a "one size fits most" mentality. Flexibility in dates, times, and location will be critical to the viability of the church in a digital age.

But it's not just the collapse of sacred Sunday schedules that challenges the analog church. It's people's physical distance from our church communities. In a trend accelerated by the growth of Airbnb, Vrbo, and other digital travel sites, which connect travelers to customized and often elaborate travel opportunities, many are spending more of the weekend on the road. This trend accelerated and perhaps solidified during the pandemic, when travelers traded lengthy air travel vacations for nearby weekend road trips.[27] With Americans taking fewer and fewer vacation days from their place of employment, it's likely that two-hundred-mile weekend road trips will become the de facto standard for the American vacation experience.[28]

As travel habits evolve, millennials and, to some extent, Generation Z are taking advantage of the "gig economy" in a quasi-nomadic lifestyle involving frequent travel and regular remote work. Supported by gig economy hubs like Upwork and Fiverr, young Americans are less committed to a permanent mailing address and more committed to flexible living. One in three Americans now works as a remote employee (without an office) or a freelancer (without a day-to-day employer), a percentage that is expected to accelerate in a postpandemic landscape.[29] Not every young adult will opt for a consistently transient lifestyle, but impermanence will redefine neighborhoods of the digital age.

In the era of the analog church, the office-based structure of workplaces and schools tethered workers—churches' members—to a specific geographic community. These individuals put down roots and became stable members in established faith communities. In the digital age, mobility will make us less inclined to become members of a church for the long term. In turn, these trends will make us more inclined to participate in the collaborative work of hybrid faith communities, where mission and ministry are available online and offline, synchronously and asynchronously. In the digital age, we may join a church in our temporary geographic neighborhood. Whether we stay with that church will depend on our ability to connect with the congregation asynchronously and digitally, to remain connected to the community whenever our circumstances change.

THE CHURCH WE WERE

The analog church embraced a form of community that was defined by predictable schedules, well-maintained facilities, and face-to-face forms of togetherness. Largely disconnected from the digital world, our previous way of being church saw the web as a high-tech bulletin board, a place with information about community gatherings that were happening offline.

As we will see in the coming chapter, the digitally distributed church we became in the Covid-19 pandemic was better at accompanying individuals in digital spaces, but it saw an erosion of the social ties that were so crucial to—and the strength of—the analog church. And because it struggled to create and strengthen social ties, the church that we became was less capable at forming individuals and communities for faithful service.

As it turns out, that last coffee hour before the Covid-19 pandemic was about far more than doughnuts. On March 15, 2020, I couldn't have imagined that over a year and a half would pass before I could once again enjoy a cup of coffee with church friends, before I could check in with other new parents in the congregation, before I could bounce around ideas for technology in the church with the church media team. I couldn't have imagined that we'd wait so long before we could once again casually chat about the sermon with pastors who knew everyone in the congregation on a first-name basis.

That last coffee hour continues to remind me that we must never relinquish the strong social fabric experienced through the prepandemic, analog church. The Digital Reformation will change much about Christian community, but we must find a way to preserve the ties that bind us together in Christian love, to keep the connections that form us to serve our neighbor.

2

THE FIRST YouTube BAPTISM

THE DIGITAL-ONLY CHURCH

My daughter was baptized in front of a live studio audience. Or at least that is how it felt at the time. With the baptism originally scheduled for April 26, 2020, we were forced by the pandemic to reschedule the sacrament three times. The waters we had collected from favorite lakes across Wisconsin had remained in our freezer for several months, remaining near a tub of orange sherbet and a bag of frozen corn kernels.

Finally, after seven months of shuttered sanctuaries, many area congregations, including ours, decided to reopen for limited-attendance baptisms, funerals, and weddings. We eagerly reserved a new date—Sunday, November 8—and invited a small list of guests. Our parents and siblings would join the pastor, the video producer, and the sound manager in the church building. The baptism would be recorded and stitched into the following Sunday's worship livestream. It would be among the first YouTube baptisms for our congregation, one

41

of many milestones our community would celebrate from a distance during the Covid-19 pandemic.

That Sunday was the first time my family had walked through the doors of our church building since the last coffee hour on March 8. Long accustomed to encountering greeters who offered handshakes and bulletins, we were met instead with sign-in sheets and hand sanitizer dispensers. After the pastor took our temperature via a touchless thermometer and wrote down our contact information for tracing purposes, we each washed our hands and walked into an unrecognizable sanctuary.

What had long been a large sanctuary with over five hundred chairs for worship attendees, and a play area for small children, had been transformed into a high-end recording studio. Cords and cables ran across the floor, taped down in rows where we used to sit on Sunday mornings. High-definition cameras, professional sound mixing boards, and even a green screen occupied the space where the back row of chairs once sat. Light reflectors blocked one set of steps leading up to the altar. A box of costumes and props for recorded children's sermons and vacation Bible school lessons sat in what had been the center aisle. The staff had also moved the baptismal font toward the back of the room, which I later learned was to facilitate a higher-quality recording. Leaving the font near the altar would have made it more difficult to capture the words of promise spoken by Annie and me as parents and by the baptismal sponsors.

The pastor invited the baptismal party to stand in front of a dozen or so chairs, spaced six feet apart, each occupied by a masked family member. Noting the new social distancing protocols of the ritual, she explained where we and the sponsors should stand for the ceremony. I set up my laptop and initiated a Zoom call with my brother, who would join from his home in Berlin, Germany.

Our media director provided a countdown. The lights were turned up, the cameras rolled, and the baptism began. We had started to confess our faith through the words of the Apostles' Creed, and for a moment, all felt familiar for a fairly typical Lutheran baptism service. Until someone noticed that a crucial wire was unplugged, a wire that connected the recorded video to the software that created the livestream. The media director called "cut!" He plugged in the wire, double-checked the connections, and we started again.

By the grace of God and the media savvy of our church's technology team, our daughter was baptized into the life, death, and resurrection of Jesus, sealed by the Holy Spirit and marked with the cross of Christ forever. The community of our Madison, Wisconsin, congregation welcomed our daughter that morning into the mission we all share as people of faith.

Our small assembly of close family applauded. The lights dimmed, and the red recording indicator faded. Our daughter then decided to splash around in the font, throwing the holy water across the room's burgundy carpet, delighting in that living water. With our families, we left the sanctuary for a socially distanced picnic celebration, reveling in the uncharacteristic warmth of an early November Sunday.

The following Sunday, 350 church members, friends, and family gathered in living rooms and kitchens to watch the baptism as part of the 9:00 a.m. livestream. Some watched from the communities of Madison, Verona, and Fitchburg, Wisconsin, where most of our church members reside.

Others tuned in from Arizona and Florida, viewing the service from homes in communities that are annual havens for Wisconsin retirees fleeing the snow. A few, like my brother and his wife, tuned in internationally. Reclined on our living room couch, exactly a five-minute drive from the building where the service had taken place just a week before, our little family watched the baptism together. I noticed that our one-year-old daughter was clearly perplexed at that moment, no doubt wondering how she had come to be on the television screen. It occurred to me how unaware she must be of the magical confluence of church streaming software, YouTube, and a television with a Google Chromecast plugged into the HDMI outlet.

The church we became during the Covid-19 pandemic was a digitally distributed church, and the location of our life together was almost exclusively online. The church we became allowed us to safely get through the pandemic. It also extended the reach of our congregation into new communities. Still, the experience left something to be desired. The personal connections we had last experienced in March 2020 were noticeably lacking; the opportunities to get involved were less consistent and more restricted. The church we became was markedly better at inviting individuals to observe the life of the congregation. Yet the lack of connection and cohesion and the shared sense of isolation limited what we could do to build up one another for lives of faithful service. Adept at inviting but poor at equipping, the church experience of the Covid-19 pandemic showed us the promise of a digitally integrated faith community while reminding us that the work of the church will likely never be entirely virtual.

During this time of digital distribution, I worked with a few congregations to explore what online worship, faith formation, and church leadership might look like. Inevitably, each conversation started with a focus on technology and virtual church—the tactical questions. What apps and resources can I use to create connections? What websites and blogs share the best ideas for keeping the congregation together? Other questions were aspirational. What would online church community ideally look like? How could we stay truly connected asynchronously? Yet most conversations eventually segued into a lament on the disintegration of the church community. How can we get through this? What can we do to prevent members of our community, particularly those unaccustomed to constant digital connection, from feeling isolated from one another? Every church leader seemed to acknowledge they had something to gain from improving the virtual experience of their programming while simultaneously recognizing that even the highest levels of digital expertise could go only so far. Perhaps, though only intuitively, they understood that social distancing prevented the forming and strengthening of the weak ties that were so crucial to the analog church.

I remain an advocate of technology in the church because I believe that thoughtfully deployed digital tools are the best way to extend the widest possible invitation, the ideal foundation for building a collaborative church culture for a digital age. But those conversations during the peak early months of the pandemic challenged my thinking. I left them somewhat skeptical, even a little jaded, about what technology could and could not do in a Christian community. Gradually I became certain that the future of Christianity would have to be a blend of the online and the offline. The exclusively virtual church would remain a rarity.

THE RAPID RISE OF THE ONLINE CHURCH

In the spring of 2020, church community in most contexts was exclusively virtual. Yet it's difficult to know exactly how many churches went online during the pandemic, more difficult still to know how many participated in worship online. The data, at best, are fragmentary. The leading worship streaming platforms, Facebook and YouTube, tally a video "view" after just a few seconds of viewership. This means that someone who pauses midscroll on Facebook to watch thirty seconds of a worship service would technically count as a "view" and thus as a virtual worship participant. Some of what Facebook and YouTube counted as virtual worship attendance was more of a virtual worship "glance"—the equivalent of approaching a church building, looking through the windows, and then driving past. My family certainly experienced Sundays where a tired toddler, a sink full of dishes, or an unexpected knock on the door from friends and family led us to stop the livestream minutes into the service. This has created uncertainty around tracking and measurement, although congregations, denominations, and others have tried to come up with useful, credible numbers. For example, the ELCA Office of the Secretary, responsible for gathering a variety of membership statistics, instructs congregations to add the number of video views to the number of digital downloads, then multiply by two to account for family viewership.[1]

Still, a large set of survey data indicates the rapid and remarkably ecumenical adoption of online worship, especially during the spring and summer of 2020. Various surveys from the Barna Group, an evangelical think tank whose metrics tend to report on media-savvy evangelical churches, suggest that worship services consisting of streaming a group of leaders gathered in an empty sanctuary was quite widespread.[2] The Barna Group reported that 96 percent of pastors responding to their annual research survey had utilized livestream technologies for Sunday worship.[3] The same survey revealed that two out of three "churched adults" had watched an online service in spring 2020, causing just under half of all congregations to experience an increase in church attendance.[4]

Survey data from the Pew Research Center revealed similar trends. According to Pew, churchgoers were quick to change the "channel" of their church attendance, from in-person services prior to March 13 to online services beginning March 15. Eighty-two percent of regular churchgoers participated in online worship in the early months of the pandemic. Just 12 percent of churchgoers attended churches that did not offer online worship. The rapid switch to online worship attendance could explain, in part, why 35 percent of Christians and even 11 percent of religious nones found their faith strengthened during the early weeks of the coronavirus outbreak.[5]

So while the specific numbers are somewhat fragmented, we can say that the rise of online worship was rapid indeed. With Easter 2020 occurring just weeks after the start of the pandemic, many churches measured record attendance for Easter Sunday. Some churches even noticed record attendance on Christmas Eve 2020, demonstrating the vitality of online church community throughout the pandemic.

These numbers tell an intriguing story about agility and capacity for innovation within the church. Few if any other organizations were so quick at converting their services and programming to a digitally distributed format. What the numbers don't explain is why digital worship was so quick to catch on. What made digital worship so desirable during spring 2020 and beyond?

For years, leaders have nudged faith communities toward evangelism or outreach, reminding those gathered to "tell your friends" and "bring them to church." But the invitational character of the church has been about more than mere words. Faith communities have developed practices and processes of hospitality, ensuring not just that invitations would be sent but that a genuine welcome would be extended to all who accepted the invitation. Churches have developed hospitality committees; added greeters and welcome notepads and words of welcome at the start of the service; prayed for guests during the prayers of the people; and sought out guests after the service, thanking them for attending, offering to answer any questions about the life of the community, and sending them home with gift bags. Hybrid ministry extends this invitational character into digital spaces.

The digital church capitalizes on long-standing invitational sentiments within the tradition, using technology to connect with those who may not have had easy access to the analog church. The streaming of services on Facebook created an opportunity for individuals to attend church via the very routine act of logging on to social media. Televising worship during the pandemic created an opportunity for individuals to connect via the ubiquitous act of sitting on one's couch and turning on the TV. On Sunday mornings, Instagram users caught glimpses of sermon feeds in the midst of a "Sunday Scroll," while digital readings and reflections provided access to the Scriptures without so much as a walk over to one's bookshelf.

One of the more intriguing examples of being invitational came from Nadia Bolz-Weber, a Lutheran pastor, author, and storyteller. Bolz-Weber posted a series of Sunday prayers to Instagram each Sunday throughout the pandemic. Honest and heartfelt, the prayers asked God for guidance and grace through the challenges of isolation in a time of crisis. Some of Bolz-Weber's posts were comical, praying for patience with the Grubhub driver who dropped off only one pizza instead of two, while others were quite deep, asking God for guidance in discerning one's sense of calling and vocation one year into a global catastrophe. Each of her prayers was liked tens of thousands of times and received hundreds of comments and responses.[6]

It wasn't just pastors who provided an accessible invitation. In March 2020, leadership professor and best-selling author Brené Brown hosted a series of live worship services via her Instagram page. Brown, who is not a pastor or priest but who is a devout Episcopalian, shared a fifteen-minute prayer service on her page that was attended by tens of thousands of people.[7] The success of her Instagram services demonstrated the deep longing for Christian conversation and community, even among the unchurched. I imagine that Brown's Instagram followers are predominantly followers of her academic and literary work and are not necessarily following her page for spiritual community. Nonetheless, tens of thousands showed up—because they expected to hear a message aligned with questions they were asking in that moment.

But it's not only worship and prayer that have become more accessible. Some church leaders noted a marked increase in attendance at faith formation and education groups. Zoom, FaceTime, and WhatsApp made it easier to bring groups together for discussion and learning without requiring a "second commute" from home following a long day of busy family schedules, work, and school.

After I published *Grace and Gigabytes* in December 2020, I had the privilege of hosting book club discussions. Without the ability to gather in person, our discussions were held on Zoom. Each time, the church leader who convened the gathering commented that far more had showed up for the conversation than had attended past in-person book clubs. Many listened, many contributed, some were cooking dinner, some were wrangling small children, others were trying to get some work done and just wanted the conversation on in the background. Yet all were present, to the degree that they were able to participate.

Time and again, the digital character of the church we became during the pandemic bypassed the factors that limited the reach of our analog invitations. The digital tools we used to be the church connected our deep longing to share our faith with our neighbors' deep desire to experience church on their own terms, on their own schedules, and in places and formats that were accessible and convenient.

AN AWARENESS OF WHAT IS MISSING

Yet throughout all these digital interactions, it was clear that something was lacking. It might have been easier than ever to invite, gather, discuss, and worship, but even those of us who are unapologetic supporters of church technology recognized a longing to return to in-person forms of togetherness.

Unsurprisingly, surveys revealed that our communities for the most part wanted to get back together in a face-to-face setting as soon as possible. When asked to predict their postpandemic worship plans, just 2 percent of respondents planned to primarily attend worship online.[8] Most of those surveyed indicated that they would participate in online events at prepandemic levels as soon as it was safe to resume large, public assemblies.[9]

Digital forms of church may be easy, but they appear to lack the analog church's capacity for forming ties and equipping for service. So why is it that the church we were during the pandemic struggled to connect and equip their communities? And what might that say about our future in digital spaces?

While digital forms of church extend a far-reaching invite that connects communities in ways that were previously unimaginable, these connections are often passive instead of participatory. The mode of digital connection experienced during the pandemic created many opportunities for viewership and for voicing ideas but provided few opportunities to experience the embodied aspects of liturgy: kneeling in the pews, standing for the gospel, singing a hymn, or tasting bread and wine. Nor did this mode of digital connection offer opportunities to actively contribute to worship leadership: to sing, to pray, to announce, or to preside. Most congregations streamed their services to some combination of YouTube, Facebook, or Zoom. Of these three, only Zoom is equipped for multidirectional conversation. YouTube and Facebook allow for comments and reactions but provide limited opportunities for back-and-forth interaction. Media-savvy churches have augmented their streaming feed with high-end broadcast software like OBS Studio or Vimeo Livestream, applications that facilitate higher quality production with features like the ability to switch between multiple camera angles or to include song lyric overlays.

Yet even these ministries have found few opportunities to get individuals meaningfully involved in worship leadership. If anything, these platforms worsened the problem, adding more style and polish to online worship and reinforcing the perception that Sunday morning was the work of professionalized pastors and broadcast technology experts. In this way, streaming technologies remind me of smoke machines, electric guitars, and laser light shows in church "auditoriums." They create a visually compelling production but do not encourage people with diverse voices and perspectives to contribute to the shared experience of liturgy. These platforms were unable to create a collaborative worship experience that was truly "the work of the people," wherein many are involved in each aspect of worship, from ushering to serving Communion. In the in-person church, some members led and served, many did not, but all had the opportunity to become involved.

Many leaders tested innovative ways to get more people involved with Sunday morning. Some added virtual lectors, recording readings during the week and stitching them into the Sunday livestream. Others recorded children's messages and sermons from a contextually relevant location such as a garden or vineyard, while some invited a member of the congregation to read the week's announcements during the broadcast. Some provided opportunities to contribute prerecorded music, editing recordings of individuals into virtual choirs and bands. All of these increased worshippers' involvement and therefore should not be discounted. The challenge, however, is that these efforts created opportunities for only a fraction of the overall community. Comparing a volunteer schedule of any prepandemic Sunday to the list of contributors to an online service shows just how few were actually invited to contribute. Some larger congregations saw the numbers of their volunteers reduced from dozens—or in the case of megachurches, hundreds—to just a few individuals, usually those with specific technical expertise. For the vast majority who never had an opportunity to be a virtual lector, musician, or preacher, there was little to differentiate the passive experience of the worship broadcast from any other digital video content.

I felt the passive nature of online worship most when I was in the pulpit. Preaching to an empty sanctuary is no easy task. It's impossible to tell if a message truly lands. Missing are the head nods, smiles, and other reactions that create a slight but significant feedback loop every time a preacher shares a message. To complicate matters, even the most well-timed jokes are inevitably met with silence or the sound of polite, muffled laughter from the few who are involved with the recording or broadcast. On the occasions when I preached a sermon on YouTube or Facebook, I knew many were or would be watching at home. I even recognized that some of my social media connections who never go to church likely tuned in to catch a few seconds of my message. But as any preacher who stepped into the virtual pulpit can attest, something was clearly missing. Those sermons showed me that even reading and preaching, which are in and of themselves one-directional communications, are meant to be collaborative experiences. The connections one experiences with the congregation when preaching in the pulpit, reading at the lectern, or presiding behind the altar are in fact collaborative experiences, the reactions and expressions of the community shaping the tone and direction of the liturgy. That sense of connection leads, inevitably, to the ever-important ties within a faith community.

Small but significant moments of collaboration are what we missed out on in the virtual church, whether those connections took place in the lobby over hot beverages or in the sanctuary during an hour of prayer. Still, we know the invitational quality of digital worship is valuable. And if that value is important to us, we'll find a way to retain it. The question is, how do we preserve the most critical aspects of digital worship without losing the connections and collaboration afforded through face-to-face community?

THE VIRTUAL CHURCH PACKING LIST

The list of practices that must be preserved from exclusively virtual church is brief. In fact, it includes only two items: easy access and a front-row seat for everyone.

Public worship, or an encounter with the grace of Jesus, is essential to the Christian tradition, and streaming is the best tool for extending such an encounter into the digital age. The one-click accessibility of a service streamed to Facebook, shared live on Instagram, or published to YouTube creates a perpetual open door to community members that is unmatched by even the most thoughtful building designs. Wherever we travel as part of the Digital Reformation, we must remain committed to the public accessibility digital tech provides. This is, in fact, the great missional opportunity of our time. Congregations that disconnect from the internet and retreat into the walls of the sanctuary place limits on the public character of Christian worship.

Some communities will unplug from virtual. This is unsurprising. Digital connections in the church are resource intensive, particularly for small parishes with limited budgets and staff resources.

Digital connections in the church require equipment, from cameras and microphones in the sanctuary to video conferencing systems in the classroom. They demand expertise to work the camera, the soundboard, the Zoom account, and the streaming software. They require maintenance, from occasional software installations and system reboots to repairs of hardware and other technical infrastructure. These are significant challenges in the American church, where, according to a 2012 Duke University study, the average congregation had only seventy active members and an annual budget of $85,000.[10]

Even with all this work, often these digital connections don't actually connect with anyone. Nobody watches, nobody joins the Zoom, nobody downloads the recording or listens to the podcast of the sermon audio. It's not uncommon for any YouTube video to get fewer than ten views, for blogs to never be seen, for social media posts to generate no activity.[11] As we journey onward in the Digital Reformation, these realities will challenge our commitment to invitational, virtual church. These challenges will tempt us to unplug and will require us to remain steadfast in our commitment to preserving online faith community—even in those moments when nobody is watching.

Of course, it's not just the ease of access to worship that we should seek to retain from the church we were during the pandemic. What made the digital church distinctive during the pandemic was not just that it was invitational or accessible. Rather, what made it distinctive from the prepandemic church is that we provided the digital attendee, the virtual worshipper, or the online contributor with the metaphorical "front-row seat." We redesigned our community life for a virtual-first experience. In many congregations, gone were the zoomed-out camera angles from the back of the balcony. Gone were the patchy audio feeds for those joining remotely in committee meetings. These low-quality experiences were replaced with camera angles from the front of the pews, with Zoom calls that gave us all equal standing in the conversation, and with words of welcome that specifically addressed those gathered in cyberspace.

However our hybrid future unfolds, we are called to preserve this front-row experience for those gathered online. This will be an immense logistical challenge. Few will want lighting equipment and video cameras obstructing their view from the pews. Some change-averse community members, when seated in the pews, will not want to see video screens on the walls, let alone watch a virtual sermon or children's message. But it's not just digital skeptics that we must be concerned with. We should also be attentive to our time and energy. As church leaders, we won't want to simultaneously serve as preacher and videographer. Trying to deal with time-consuming technologies even as we attend to the already significant responsibility of presiding and preaching in person is often unrealistic and usually unwise. Many leaders already take on a list of tasks well beyond the scope of a pastor's responsibilities to the ministry of Word and sacrament: greeting attendees, checking in volunteers, refilling the coffeepots, and exchanging pleasantries as worshippers file out of the building.

Still, if we remain committed to hybrid forms of ministry, if we believe in the missional opportunities of the digital age, then we must address the demands digital ministry places on resources and time. The accessibility of digital church, and the front-row seat afforded by digital connections, must remain central to our life together as we venture into our hybrid future. Hybrid ministry will necessitate not just digital skills but a commitment to the significance of online ministry to our mission and vision.

HOW TO BUILD DIGITAL COMMUNITY

Until this point in the book, we've thought about the Digital Reformation as a progression toward a hybrid of offline and online or a form of ministry that blends the best of analog and digital connections. While I would argue that hybrid ministry is the best method for our life together in a digital age, it is not the only model. Some will continue to explore whether a Christian community can survive, and even thrive, on exclusively digital connections.

Several models exist for this type of ministry. The first forms of exclusively online church existed through Second Life, a free application where avatars interacted in a lifelike "3D virtual world." It was there that the Anglican Cathedral of Second Life originated, bringing a community of predominantly Episcopalians together for liturgy, prayer, and study. While the Anglican Cathedral continues to gather on Second Life, other Second Life worshipping communities have dwindled as the platform has become less popular. Following the lead of

Second Life churches like the Anglican Cathedral, other ministers have begun to experiment with church in virtual reality. In *Grace and Gigabytes*, for example, I shared the story of Pastor D. J. Soto, a virtual reality enthusiast who started a congregation that meets entirely in VR. Members create avatars and join the community for weekly worship and daily community life using an easily available headset like an Oculus Rift. Soto sees the VR church as intrinsically inclusive, open to all regardless of one's beliefs, and sees an opportunity for authentic Christian connection in a space where participants are not asked to conform to a church's established norms.

As church planters continue to experiment with exclusively online forms of church community, they may become constrained by the hardware necessary to create and particpate in virtul reality events. The more prevalent model will likely be a combination of social media, digital content, and occasional synchronous connection. As big tech platforms evolve, resources like Facebook groups may become hubs for ministry experiments. Facebook groups offer communities the opportunity to gather on message boards for conversation and on Facebook Messenger for video calls. They provide technology for streaming live video content and sharing recorded audio. There are even tools for processing donations and offerings within a Facebook group. And for better or for worse, big tech is investing significant resources in developing and strengthening these groups. Mark Zuckerberg, the CEO of Facebook, sees "meaningful groups," or hubs of daily interaction, as the future of social media. Zuckerberg and Facebook plan to invest billions of dollars in creating meaningful connections via groups with a goal of one billion regular group users by the year 2023.[12] Earlier, we described how pages about spirituality and religion rank among the most viewed group categories on Facebook. It's only a matter of time before these spaces attempt to make the jump from informal communities to established congregations.

Still, there are many challenges facing an exclusively virtual form of church. Perhaps the most significant challenge is the transience of social media communities. Congregations thrive on the weak ties that are established through momentary yet consistent interactions. Even as active church members spend an average of less than ten minutes a day on spiritual and church-based activities, they still return to church on a near-weekly basis. Engagement with Facebook groups and other digital communities is highly erratic. With over one billion Facebook groups and hundreds of millions of organizational Facebook pages from businesses, schools, nonprofits, and churches, the market for digital community is heavily saturated. I myself am a member of over forty Facebook groups. Yet though I may be a regular user of Facebook, I rarely visit any of these groups. At the time of this writing, I had visited just one group, a community for staff alumni of Crossways Camping Ministries, in the past month. With so many communities to choose from, users will join and leave church communities with a single click of the mouse. Digital church communities are therefore unlikely to see enough consistent involvement from their community members and, consequently, may find it difficult to collaborate or to equip individuals for service to the neighbor.

Content quality presents another core challenge to an exclusively digital faith community. Without an established, face-to-face relationship, users will demand a high level of quality in our digital audio, video, and social posts, as well as a predictable cadence for the publication of this content. Most of us lack the digital media savvy of established videographers and professional audio producers. This may be less of an issue for evangelical leaders, who have long demonstrated sophisticated usage of media—first radio, then television, and now the web. Mainline Protestant and Catholic leaders will have a steeper learning curve than evangelical media professionals and may find it difficult to sustain polished quality and daily consistency of digital Christian content. In an environment of content saturation, low-quality content and content that is sporadically published are often ignored.

This is not to say that exclusively digital forms of church must be abandoned. The Digital Reformation, after all, demands that we view the web as a mission field. We therefore need innovators willing to test new approaches to church community. In fact, some foundational practices can increase the likelihood that a digital community will be both inviting and equipping.

Intentional digital communities require a keen sense of contextual awareness, which can be developed by routinely asking two questions: Who do we want to invite to be a part of this community? And what type of ministry do we want to equip them for? The viability of digital church will depend on the degree to which our answers are rooted in particular needs. Creating an entirely online church intended for a broad group such as "millennials" or "the unchurched" will likely lead to frustration. As church leaders, we sometimes tend to make sweeping assumptions about online groups, which make it more challenging to connect with them. That's why digital community follows a process of convening, uplifting, and sustaining. We effectively convene digital community only where we have a clear sense of why such a community exists and whom it seeks to connect with. We cannot get to a place of shared encounter without convening conversations that involve deep listening. This deep listening leads us into an awareness of a group's shared affinities and passions, which in turn helps us create content and experiences that are relevant and compelling.

Once established, online communities connect through shared specific affinities, which are reflected in the community's conversations, content, and programming. Members of these communities could be residents of a specific geographic neighborhood or members of a certain demographic or psychographic group—for example, politically progressive working parents who want to connect to a faith community but can't find the time to fit church into their busy family schedules. They could be any individual who shares an affinity for a niche topic, such as yoga-based faith practices or Lectio divina readings. Predominantly online ministry must recognize the specific shared interests of digital communities, just as they would recognize the specific attributes of a physical neighborhood. We uplift our communities when the content and cadence of communal life resonate with these specific affinities.

We also often tend to focus on equipping a digital community for something as broad as "discipleship," but again, this is too broad a concept when considered in the contextual realities of digital community. It's also based on the church's terms. Communities may not be interested in being "equipped for discipleship." But they may be intrigued by spiritual guidance and communal accompaniment through a major life transition. Or they might find it compelling to join a group that provides support groups and faith-based programming in response to a specific health challenge or diagnosis. Whatever the premise of the group, digital faith communities that manage to perpetuate their ministry will be precise. It is only through this deep sense of contextual awareness that a digital faith community can withstand the transience, saturation, and distractibility that often defines our online existence.

Once a community is convened and the connections are uplifted through engaged participants, it is sustained whenever community members share or invite others into the life of the group. We are inspired to share about groups or communities that speak meaningfully to our joys, longings, and losses. A generic faith-based community may not spread. A group that is anchored in its specific context may not spread to many, but those who find it will be all the more likely to participate, contribute, and even lead. However we choose to go about building a digital faith community, we begin from this foundation of awareness and attunement to real human beings, who just happen to gather online.

WHICH WAY TO LOOK?

In the church we became during the pandemic, I never knew quite where to look—what to physically watch. On the day my daughter was baptized, I didn't know whether we should be looking at her, the close relatives scattered at six-foot increments around the font, or the steady red camera light at the back of the church. On the occasions when I was invited to preach to a digitally distributed audience, I found myself wanting to use the "pan and scan" eye-gaze technique that many preachers and speakers are familiar with. I found myself wanting to make eye contact with those who had once sat in our sanctuary. As I began to preach, my eyes anxiously scanned the room, yet nobody was there. Not having a background in acting or film, I felt uncomfortable looking straight into the camera, and looking to the side of the sanctuary where the studio lighting equipment was positioned was distracting.

Most of the time, we are on the other side of the screen, the other side of the camera. On every Zoom call, meeting, and book study, each webinar and discussion group I joined, I never quite figured out how to convey that I was closely engaged with the conversation. Every time I tried to reference something on my screen, I noticed that I looked like I was trying to multitask, to deal with another item on my to-do list via another browser tab or app. I also often wonder what the hours upon hours of seeing ourselves mirrored back on a Zoom call, hours many of us inevitably spent scrutinizing our appearance as we attempted to look both focused and presentable, will do to our self-esteem!

The uncertain gaze of the exclusively online church is but one marker of the challenges and promise of digital faith communities. On the one hand, connections seem less meaningful, our relationships lacking a sense of depth. On the other hand, the abundance of online connections makes it easier to hear the concerns from the community beyond our sanctuaries. These connections help us fix our gaze beyond the four walls to more intentionally engage the needs of the neighbor.

Defined by its contradictions, the digital church is a rather passive experience for many. But it is also the most accessible form of church we have ever come up with. No longer limited to a specific geography, it is a truly ambiguous form of faith community, yet it is also the form of ministry with by far the greatest reach. And although it lacks the feedback loops and the light conversations that create such meaningful bonds in the analog church, digital faith community provides access to diverse and varied perspectives, creating opportunities for dialogue and collaborative service we once would have never imagined.

Hybrid ministry is a method of working through these tensions, of leaning into these contradictions. There is nothing we can do to imbue our interactions in cyberspace with the same enriching content of our face-to-face interactions, just as there is nothing we can come up with that will make our analog experiences as accessible and inviting as our virtual encounters. That's why the Digital Reformation is a movement toward a hybrid form of ministry that builds on the best from the analog and the digital. The church we were and the church we became during the pandemic struggle to be both inviting and equipping. The church we must become will work through the opportunities and shortcomings of both experiences to create the optimum blend of online and offline. We now turn to that hybrid future, with a commitment to invite and to equip, to gather and to guide, in a time of experimentation and uncertainty.

THE NEXT EASTER

EMERGING HYBRID CHURCH COMMUNITY

Annie and I sat at the kitchen table on the dreary Easter morning of 2020, eating brunch and enjoying a postvirtual worship mimosa. The day had started like no other Easter Sunday. In place of brass quintets and crowded churches without a parking spot to be found, we watched, experienced, and participated in a worship livestream cast to our television, noting our uncertainty about how to refer to online worship. In place of sharing a meal with dozens of close relatives, we chatted on a Zoom call. Still, at just a few weeks into the pandemic, the novelty of online connection had yet to wear off. We were eager to attend church and see our family, even if on a screen.

We had dressed up for the occasion, clearing off the table and setting two places. We had even prepared a full Easter brunch featuring the traditional egg dishes and baked goods, trimmed with the necessary jelly beans and chocolate rabbits—altogether far more food than two adults and one

THE HOLY AND THE HYBRID

baby could possibly consume. We logged off the postbrunch family call to an uncommon stillness. With our five-month-old napping in another room, the silence of our kitchen was interrupted only by the soft hum of the overhead lighting. "At least it won't be like this at the next Easter," I said in a voice of naive confidence as I helped myself to a second scone. "Things will surely be back to normal by then." Annie nodded in agreement, likely not sharing all of my unfounded optimism.

In a sense, I was correct. The next Easter wasn't completely like the Easter that took place on that early pandemic Sunday when the world felt so suddenly unfamiliar. It also wasn't completely like the Easters we had been accustomed to every other year of our lives. As it turns out, the next Easter was an in-between occasion, a liminal moment situated between the isolation of the past year and the promise of togetherness on the other side of widespread vaccination. That Easter reminded us of the importance of gathering, which raised the possibility that these gatherings might never again resemble what we had experienced before the pandemic.

It was April 2021, and the long, dark pandemic winter had given rise to brightening spring. With dry, sunny weather and a drop in local case counts, our congregation was ready to open on Easter Sunday for an in-person, outdoor service. It would be the first public worship gathering since the early onset of winter had halted the outdoor services of October and early November. It would also begin the first phase of a building reopening plan, a series of small steps that would gradually open the doors of our sanctuary.

Church members had several viewing options that Easter morning: attend the socially distant outdoor service, watch the livestreamed service online, or watch a previously assembled and recorded service online or on local television. The following weekend, the second Sunday of Easter, members would be able to participate in a limited-attendance indoor service at one of the church's campuses. The weekend after that, they could choose between capacity-limited services at either of the church's two buildings.

In defining that Eastertide plan, the congregation's reopening task force had acknowledged a guiding concept for the church we must become: that some members were longing to return to the building, that some wanted to remain online, and that many were uncertain about where and how they wanted to worship. Whether the task force realized it, the split between those wanting to return and those desiring to stay online will remain with us even after the worst of the pandemic has ended. In the context of the Digital Reformation, differences in vaccination status and risk tolerance are just one of the many factors that influence how we participate in Christian community. Individuals and families will continue to make ongoing calculations about whether that community is best experienced in analog or digital forms. Just as we once started our Sundays deciding what attire was suitable to wear to church, we will soon start our Sundays deciding whether online or in-person worship is most suitable for the personal and situational realities of a given moment.

THREE POSSIBILITIES

As church leaders, we might respond to this ongoing consideration with three possible approaches to hybrid ministry in a tech-shaped culture. First, some of us might desire to follow customary practices in an effort to remain faithful to long-held values about what the church is called to be and do. This first approach, characterized by a de-prioritization of the digital, retains the way we've done church for decades. This approach doesn't require additional resources or staffing. Unplugging from the web also implies a commitment to more intentional forms of togetherness. It is easy to lose focus and begin to multitask during a Zoom worship service. There are simply fewer distractions and demands on our focus in the analog church. The decision to unplug in the late-pandemic or postpandemic church (or to remain unplugged), which will likely be more common among smaller churches and multipoint parishes that are unable to invest in the infrastructure required for hybrid ministry, likely emanates from discussions about resources and ministry priorities. Circumstances might dictate that this is the most realistic path, even if it may not be the ideal one.

Unfortunately, this position doesn't take advantage of what we have learned about being church in digital spaces. It deletes from the working memory of our church culture all that we have discovered about using the web to be invitational and inclusive. The lost learning is not the greatest problem with this option, however. The greatest consequence of unplugging is that we relinquish the missional opportunities of online ministry. We let go of the opportunity to connect with members who are unable to attend in person, whether due to physical ailment or disability or perhaps past traumatic experiences in a church setting. We let go of the chance to engage with nonmembers from our surrounding community; we forfeit our presence in the digital spaces where our communities spend multiple hours each day.

We may make the decision to unplug after seeing relatively low levels of engagement with digital content and programming. With comparatively few regular churchgoers planning to attend church exclusively online, we are likely to see a drop-off in digital activity in our "new normal," if we have not already experienced such a drop-off.[1] However, this is not a sign that we should disconnect. The goal of our presence in digital spaces is not to create digital experiences that are viewed in great numbers. Rather, the goal is to accompany communities in day-to-day digital life. So while it's true that digital ministry has a cost, in terms of both dollars and effort, there is a cost of unplugging that is calculated not in dollars but in the ability to be online, where our communities are often found. This cost may turn out to be much greater than the savings that accrue from canceling subscriptions to software and returning hardware and equipment.

Second, we might offer an online alternative to in-person community, perhaps including a worship livestream or an occasional video discussion group. Perhaps because of financial constraints, a congregation might livestream or record worship using one camera at the back of the sanctuary, capturing the backs of people's heads and distancing the online viewer from the service. Adult forums might enable online learners to hear the words of a teacher but not to hear (or to hear clearly) the contributions of in-person learners—nor to join the conversation. One might participate in worship online, but they are unable to fill worship leadership roles, greet other members, or offer prayer requests. Whether in worship, faith formation, or fellowship, the virtual experience within this model is passive, not participatory.

This model may be the most common of all. Although creating this type of digital community requires resource- and energy-intensive effort, it does not require that we reinvent the community. This model will be especially enticing for small- and medium-sized churches whose leaders are weary after guiding their communities through a time of digital distribution. The positive aspect of this model is that it creates an easy digital entry point into the life of the congregation without requiring the congregation to significantly adapt its practices or overhaul its technologies. The church that offers digital as an alternative also preserves the intentionality of in-person connection, just as a fully analog church might do. The digital-alternative church might be appreciated by individuals who are unavailable on a given Sunday morning.

Of course, the model of online as an alternative has some drawbacks. Without intentional efforts to actively involve online participants, the digital experience can become a "second tier" membership, a lesser status than that of those who choose to travel to the building on Sundays and throughout the week. It is also not a model conducive to connecting the broader congregation, in that it creates for online and offline silos. Those who watch online will tend to remain connected to those who are predominantly online, assuming they connect with anyone at all, while those who attend in person will predominantly interact with others who are also in person. This is the model of a fragmented church, where those online and those offline feel like they are part of two separate congregations.

The third model is a full and participatory integration of the online and the offline. This bridge between online and offline is the root of the hybrid church, the greatest opportunity of the Digital Reformation. In worship, an online participant leads the prayer. In a council meeting, a digital attendee facilitates the conversation. In classes, online learners respond to discussions. In staff meetings, the senior pastor leads the discussion via video conferencing. With this model, we offer digitally enabled experiences not out of some desire to be trendy or to plug into a church leadership trend but to develop a truly collaborative church culture, one that continually broadens the opportunity to contribute to mission.

Recognizing that individuals may find themselves on both sides of the bridge from week to week and in different seasons of one's life, we should do everything we can to ensure parity of online and offline experiences in our faith community. This hybrid model has the advantage of aligning with our tech-shaped culture. In work and school, for example, we expect some degree of digital integration, so those participating virtually can actively contribute or even lead a conversation. A bridge between the online and the offline in the church conforms to this shared expectation of digital accessibility. But this model is not about mere cultural relevance. Building a bridge between the online and the offline is the best way to include all members and stakeholders in a faith community's mission. When we integrate technology, we create a collaborative church culture where everyone, online and offline, is equipped to use their gifts in service to God's call and the community's purpose.

The best part of this model is that it requires less technical aptitude than one might expect. Building a bridge between online and offline is less about how much we invest in or know about tech and more about the intention to actively involve online participants and attendees. The bridge between online and offline will be most common in churches with curious leaders who remain committed to discerning and carrying out the congregation's mission in a world of accelerating digital change.

While this is the ideal model for ministry in a postpandemic church, it is also the model with the fewest documented examples or identified best practices. We know how to isolate ourselves from digital tech. And we certainly know how to create a digital alternative to face-to-face church community, because so many churches were using this model before the pandemic. But few ministries ever would have imagined the necessity of hybrid ministry. In a sense, then, we are all starting without much of an instruction manual. Though hybrid ministry represents the best model of life together, the lack of concrete examples demands continual experimentation and iteration.

ANALOG AND DIGITAL PARITY

Recently, churches have been using the phrase "hybrid ministry" with increasing frequency. Leaders declare that reopening plans involve a hybrid format, newsletters describe a congregation's move to a hybrid model, and websites boast that a congregation is hybrid, with online and neighborhood-based campuses.

To an extent, it is encouraging to see the growth of this concept in church leadership circles. Yet when a word or phrase rapidly increases in usage within church settings, it tends to lose its shared meaning. As an example, look at "innovation," the buzzword spoken at every conference, in every seminary, and at each denominational gathering prior to the pandemic. We've hired directors of innovation and brought in consultants to create innovation strategies. We've read books and attended talks and created task forces. Amid this overuse, Christian innovation has developed many different and often conflicting definitions.

We don't need a textbook definition of hybrid ministry so much as we need an understanding of what is essential to its practice. And the key ingredient for hybrid ministry isn't what one might think. It's not that our church is online. It's not that we stream services or that we conduct meetings or classes using video calls or that we communicate through messaging applications. Rather, the key ingredient of hybrid ministry is parity between the online and the offline experience. If we are truly doing hybrid ministry, there is no meaningful difference between connecting online and in person.

Parity of experience looks different depending on the setting of our experience. In worship, we once thought that all we needed for online worship was a web-enabled camera in the balcony or back row. We thought that if online viewers could see what was happening, then surely, they would feel included. But this approach to digital worship was so low quality that even I, accustomed to digital environments and committed to online community building, rarely watched. On the Sunday mornings when I did tune in to a service or sermon while road tripping or camping, I seldom remained online for more than a few moments. But it wasn't so much the positioning of the camera, dim lighting, or patchy audio that turned me away. Rather, it was the feeling that I was sitting on the outside looking in. There was no acknowledgment of the presence of online viewers—no greeting, no sense of welcome communicated through the announcements, no mentions in the prayers. I was keenly aware that I was an outsider looking in, sitting on the periphery of the community's experience.

Parity in Worship

Parity of experience in worship, then, is much more about involvement and participation than it is about production quality. This parity begins with worship planning. The process of worship planning begins with the question of what it means to worship and why individuals are gathered together around Word and sacrament. Beginning with these theological commitments, the worship planner remembers that the spirit gathers a public assembly to enact the work of the people in order to encounter the grace of God.

If a congregation assumes we worship as a public assembly, then online and offline attendees must gather in a meaningful way. From the moment the service begins, the presence and contributions of those online and offline are invited and affirmed. Planners consider how best to welcome those participating online. At a low-tech level, this involves attention to the specific language to greet those watching online. Welcoming those gathered offline and online, near and far, and remembering that we are church together sets an intention of inclusivity. Virtual participants should hear inclusive language throughout the liturgy that lifts up the gifts and concerns of the faith community wherever they are gathered.

Some hybrid ministries will go beyond inclusive language, finding a way not just to welcome and acknowledge virtual attendees but to bring them into the sanctuary. Churches using Zoom or Microsoft Teams for online worship may display the call's gallery on projection screens in the sanctuary, so the entire congregation can be in one another's presence, online and offline. Hybrid ministries will use emerging technologies to share worship leadership duties among online and analog attendees, involving worshippers no matter where they live or when they are available. Announcements can be projected and read virtually. Virtual lectors and musicians, roles utilized by many church leaders for the first time during the pandemic, will become fixtures in the hybrid church. Prayer petitions can be shared digitally.

Pastors and lay leaders might preach occasional virtual sermons, perhaps prerecorded or livestreamed from a contextually relevant site, that are then projected in the sanctuary. Video sermons were once the domain of multisite evangelical megachurches who wanted to beam the same teaching into several worship auditoriums. This could be an especially important practice in support of lay preaching, as the video format allows lay leaders to contribute to a sermon without the apprehension of speaking live to an audience of dozens or hundreds. Hybrid preaching may include a preacher in an analog pulpit who starts the sermon with twenty-second sound bites of congregants responding to a topical discussion prompt. In this sense, hybrid preaching expands the narratives in a sermon, integrating more of our experiences into the story of God's work in the congregation.

Even the weekly offering, which we associate with brass plates and wooden collection baskets, can be a hybrid event. During this point in the service, worship leaders may invite analog and digital offerings, encouraging members to use their phones to donate with a text or an app. Stewardship leaders might acknowledge the tithes and offerings shared both in the sanctuary and through digital tools, perhaps by including an additional collection plate to symbolize the contributions of those gathered online.

While the role of the worship planner is important to creating parity between the online and the offline, the role of the media team (or in small churches, the individual who knows how to use the technology) is critical to making these connections viable. Online viewers should see video and hear audio that resembles what they would see and hear in the sanctuary. This means cameras are placed in the front middle (or in multiple carefully selected locations) rather than just the far back, and audio captures words from the altar, pulpit, and the pews.

Livestreaming ought to be the primary method for online worship, in that it affords the greatest access to digital involvement. To livestream is to broadcast a service as it happens, on an accessible media platform like YouTube, Facebook, or a publicly accessible Zoom or Teams link. Livestreamed services can easily be recorded and uploaded to YouTube, Google Drive, Vimeo, or other hosting sites.

Another option is to record a service ahead of time and make it available to the community to watch on demand. Recorded worship services create some opportunities for more people to be involved. But a recorded service inevitably succumbs to the limitations experienced in the exclusively online church. Without opportunities for connection, conversation, and real-time contributions, a recorded worship service promotes a passive experience. And by providing separate experiences for online and in-person worshippers, a recorded video stymies attempts at parity. We may achieve higher production quality through a recording, but the community may fragment into online and face-to-face congregations.

However, recorded services may remain the primary medium for online worship in two cases. The first is those churches that discern their exclusive ministry site as the web. These ministries will find that a recorded worship allows for professional production quality. In a saturated ecosystem of faith-related digital content, exclusively online ministries will need to achieve this standard if their communities are to take the time to view, participate, and share with others.

Recorded services will also remain important in areas of inequitable internet access, where parishioners lack access to the digital infrastructure necessary to support livestream video. Rural congregations, churches in mountainous regions, and churches with a large percentage of members who live in long-term care facilities will far more easily connect with their parishioners through recordings (even recordings shared via DVD) than through a livestream.

Still, these experiences will be the exception rather than the norm. With recorded services offering few opportunities for seamless connection, well-integrated livestreams will emerge as the leading worship practice in the Digital Reformation.

Parity in Faith Formation

Hybrid ministry begins with worship, and parity of experience arguably matters more in worship than in any other expression of the congregation's life together. Yet parity of experience is a commitment that must be made in faith formation, church leadership, and even fellowship opportunities.

Parity of experience in hybrid worship involves connecting online and in-building attendees through livestream video. But parity of experience in education requires a different approach.

Specifically, Christian education in a digital age necessitates access to both asynchronous and live opportunities. Hybrid worship is about online and offline connections, but hybrid faith formation is about online *and/or* offline experiences.

At times, I've worked at churches that videotape classes and share the recordings with those who were unable to attend live. This has become an increasingly common practice in youth programs, where sports and other family commitments present challenges to sustained attendance. While this is a useful tool for ensuring those who are absent are not subsequently left behind, it falls short of the parity we must strive for in hybrid education.

What we're ultimately seeking in classes and education is choice: empowering learners in the community to select whether they want to be present synchronously, whether they prefer to learn independently, or whether they would like to create their own combination of online and offline, synchronous and asynchronous.

A scalable way to achieve this parity in religious education is through the sharing of curated digital resources that support asynchronous learning and inspire curiosity. For example, we might offer a member who wants to participate in a book study an invitation to join a live, in-person class, to connect to that class synchronously via Zoom, or to explore a pathway of self-paced materials that expand on the themes from the book. We might share podcasts from authors and thinkers who align with our mission and purpose, whose ideas contribute additional perspectives to the themes of the conversation. Or we might post discussion threads to social media, tagging members and encouraging them to contribute their perspectives to an online conversation.

If a church has already established a pattern of creating or curating educational content, the next opportunity is to coach community members to create materials unique to their own faith experiences. As I described in *Grace and Gigabytes*, our tech-shaped culture expects opportunities to learn by doing, to create in order to learn. This means that our role is in equal parts to create content, to curate content, and to coach our communities to create.

In a faith-formation setting, we need to create opportunities not just to learn together but to create together. The congregation becomes a setting in which we come together to craft our stories, share our stories, and listen to the stories of others. This can be done online or offline, together or independently.

Parity of experience in Christian education thus involves creating "maker spaces" for the construction of individual stories and "sharing spaces" for telling and discussing these narratives. It will become the work of the Christian educator to determine what it means to create space for crafting stories of one's faith journey online and offline and what it means to build a forum for sharing on the web and face-to-face. Whether through a discussion group and artistic activity that takes place in a church classroom or a podcast feed that broadcasts these stories to other members of the community, it is our calling to establish creative and empathetic spaces, online and offline.

Parity in Leadership

We began this section on parity of experience with worship and faith formation, since these aspects of Christian life together reach many, if not all, of the individuals within a community. We also started this section with worship and education because these require the most creativity, and perhaps the most resources. But there's one more aspect of our communal experience that deserves parity between the online and the offline. If our leaders aren't collaborating using a hybrid model, then our congregations are likely to remain analog institutions. If ordained and lay leaders don't develop a hybrid model of church administration, we are unlikely to build the bridge we are seeking; our efforts at digital ministry will remain an "alternative" to an in-person experience.

Parity of experience in church administration and leadership isn't far removed from the parity of experiences sought by corporations and nonprofits for the postpandemic workplace. As of May 2020, 63 percent of American workers worked remotely, and 54 percent of companies committed to more flexible work arrangements following the pandemic.[2] And while it's true that tech led other industries in the sudden movement toward flexible, remote-first work, they were hardly the only industry to make this pivot. A McKinsey study concluded that four out of every five managers or organizational leaders (from any industry) could work remotely with no negative impact to an organization's success.[3] The survey also found that two in three educators, one in three health care providers, and one out of five construction workers could work remotely without a loss of industry productivity or organizational effectiveness. Taken together, McKinsey estimates that at least one out of every three Americans may soon find themselves in a predominantly virtual workplace.[4]

As organizations in all industries have reimagined how they work, many have come to the realization that only a few circumstances demanded face-to-face connection. Leaders of these institutions recognize that teams can collaborate just as effectively with part-time or full-time remote work. They recognize that it would be an advantage to provide workers with flexibility and autonomy in their schedules and that asynchronous, virtual work could be just as meaningful as any tasks completed in an office. They also realized throughout the pandemic that the office could be reimagined as a place of occasional collaboration, a setting for planning and strategy conversations, but not a mandatory location for heads-down, task-oriented work. The benefits of hybrid work—which combines intentional in-office collaboration with remote, task-focused work—include higher productivity, elevated job satisfaction, and reduced infrastructure costs for the employer.

Some of us will dismiss these trends as a fad that can't possibly work in the church. After all, leaders of *those* organizations are concerned with things like productivity and profits, but aren't *we* about relationships and serving the needs of people? While it's true that productivity and effectiveness can be problematic pursuits in a church setting, this question isn't necessarily one of maximizing efficiency or improving the bottom line. In short, we shouldn't seek to create a hybrid leadership experience to get stuff done or to make money. We should attempt to create a hybrid leadership experience because it aligns with a broader cultural shift and because it exemplifies a commitment to the church's digital future.

By finding ways to do ministry work in a hybrid setting, we demonstrate that we believe virtual engagement is meaningful engagement, that true collaboration can and does happen in digital spaces. Committing to hybrid leadership practices also gives us an advantage in the talent marketplace—where we do compete for talent—positioning the church as an attractive work setting for those whose careers have long taken place in both online and offline settings.

The specifics of this transformation in church administration and leadership emanate from an understanding of what type of work is best suited for virtual and office settings. Work that is more visionary is best suited for face-to-face settings: revisiting mission, evaluating ministry models, or planning for an upcoming season in the church's life together. Work that is more task oriented should be moved to remote settings: planning a preaching series, writing a service with a planning team, or participating in a monthly meeting with the church council. As leaders of a previously analog institution, our tendency might be to try to arrange as much in-person connection as possible. We should resist this tendency by carefully scrutinizing whether face-to-face interactions will really make this work more meaningful, impactful, and productive. If we cannot discern a strong justification for meeting face-to-face, then that work is best left to web-based tools and can likely be completed asynchronously as one's own schedule allows.

Conversations around virtual work in the church inevitably turn to the minutiae: What software should we use? Should we get Slack or Microsoft Teams? How will we manage calls? Do we subscribe to Zoom and upgrade the conference room to a Zoom Room, or is teleconferencing sufficient? These are important questions and are useful to consider as we imagine the future of church leadership, both lay and ordained, in our digital age. But they are also relatively insignificant. We can create parity of experience in aspects of our church community only when our leaders, both those on staff and those who volunteer, are invested in hybrid collaboration. If we begin with that commitment and then consider the specific settings and context of our ministry and how they inform the location of our work, the technology and tactics will take care of themselves.

PERSONALIZED AND PRACTICE-BASED MINISTRY

While parity is the core ingredient of hybrid ministry, the one thing that no hybrid ministry can do without, personalization is a close runner-up. Hybrid ministries will use technology to connect individuals to shared experiences. But they will also use tech to facilitate personalized practices that edify our faith. By promoting personalized practices, hybrid ministries can use tech to achieve what exclusively online faith communities cannot: equipping people for faithful service.

Technologies that support spiritual practices allow individuals to contextualize the messages they are hearing through worship and faith formation and to apply them to their everyday life. These resources are personalized because they align with specific individual needs. They are practice based because they invite the individual to create a space for core Christian disciplines of prayer, Scripture study, and contemplation.

These resources need not be digitally sophisticated. A custom church app that uses push notifications to remind us to read Scripture, breathe, and express gratitude at times of our choosing is an example of a personalized, practice-based technology. But it is hardly the only model. Emails, social media discussions, and even text messages can support personal practices just as effectively as custom software. We may not need to create new tools to do this well. Rather, we simply need to evaluate how we can support these habits through tools we already have.

The main requirement, then, is not digital novelty but consistency and cadence. Each week, we have an opportunity to augment the messages in readings, teachings, and preaching through this personalized technology. It's important that we integrate our tech with the themes of worship and learning to facilitate a well-integrated experience. And it's important that we provide these opportunities on a predictable and repeatable schedule.

Secular organizations have been using these techniques far longer than the church. I've had firsthand experience with them. For example, 9:00 a.m. is the most stressful time of my workday. By then, I've checked my email messages, responded to new Slack posts, and scrolled through one or two news sites. When I glance at my calendar and see a day of back-to-back meetings, classes, and events, I feel the inevitable jolt of cortisol, followed up by a bit of "impostor syndrome." And so the day begins with self-scrutiny: How can I ever get all of this done? Who am I to think I can attempt to accomplish all this work?

After recognizing the predictability of these feelings, I turned to a universal human practice: gratitude. Every day at 9:00 a.m., I receive a text message that asks me to name one thing that I am grateful for. Each time that I respond, I feel a sense of calm and focus. Just taking those few seconds to disconnect and to be thankful for the opportunities and gifts in my life helps me proceed with the day with incrementally more clarity. The app, which is called Presently and is available for free on Android and iOS, keeps track of my gratitude submissions in a personalized feed, accessible only to me. I can always go back and see what I was grateful for in days, months, or years past.

It's basic technology: SMS messaging takes the items I'm grateful for and curates them in a simple list. But the impact is profound. It makes space in my life for the practice of gratitude and creates a gratitude journal. Inevitably, I still experience deadlines and long to-do lists, which brings stress and occasional frustration. But thanks to Presently, I'm more grateful and grounded.

Another helpful personal technology is one I've created. Some days my kids seem to be growing up so fast. It's difficult sometimes to keep track of the milestones, the changes, the growth. While text messages and Google Photos help me organize pictures, I find that often the fullness of a memory can't be contained within a photo. That's why I started a practice of writing down the parenting joys that I want to remember as brief stories in a Google Doc I plan to give to my kids someday. This memory practice serves as a reminder of all that is great about being a new dad and is especially powerful amid the busyness of everyday life.

I sometimes tend to forget to write down these memories, and I had often gone several weeks without recording something. That's why I downloaded Qeepsake, an app that sends me two weekly text messages with specific questions about parenting life. My answers to these questions, and some photos that I choose, go into a personal website that I can later turn into a photo book. The app asks creative yet predictable questions about what it's like to be a new parent: What gave us joy this week? What foods does she like to eat? What does she most enjoy playing with? Who does she most enjoy seeing? These short questions provide a brief spark of inspiration that in turn motivates me to write down my memories, to preserve the stories of all that is fascinating and fulfilling in being a dad. With Qeepsake, I'm able to contextualize my parenting experiences in a memorable narrative, constructing the story of our family. It's a basic app that gives me the tools I need to remember what matters most.

I have tried other practices and remain committed to some of them. For example, I'm a regular user of the Calm meditation app, which pairs well with Luther Seminary's "God Pause," a daily, lectionary-based email devotional. In my experience, a daily practice of contemplation plus Scripture readings tied to the lectionary is a necessary antidote to the harried pace of the digital age. (I fully recognize the irony that the escape from the pace of the digital is often made possible by digital tools!)

Countless other apps support many more personalized practices, and new resources are always under development. As I think about hybrid ministry, I often ask the question, What if this trend wasn't the exclusive domain of secular, quasi-self-help companies but was instead fundamental to life in Christian community? And then I ask, How can we feasibly create or recreate these resources without learning a totally new skill and investing considerable resources?

In discerning the answer to this question, it's helpful to think in terms of what tech companies label "user needs," a piece of jargon referring to existing interests within a community. For church leaders, that means we need to find out what specific spiritual or even faith-adjacent practices our communities are most interested in or are most in need of. We learn through asking questions. While we hope to integrate technology with faith-based practices, the objective is

THE NEXT EASTER

not necessarily to teach brand-new practices. Rather, it is to find a way to build and strengthen habits. So we first need to discover what sustains and nourishes the faith of individuals in your community and what distracts from an enriching spiritual life. Not every faith community will want access to mindfulness resources; not every faith community will want to consider biblical perspectives on environmental justice. But every faith community is comprised of individuals and groups with specific interests and callings. We want to use technology to build upon these sentiments.

As we ask these questions, we can seek out perspectives on when, where, and how often these practices are most feasible or most valuable. The reason personalized, practice-based technologies are effective is that they are made accessible when they are most convenient to the user. It's up to us to use technology in ways that realistically align with users' schedules and calendars. If we find that most of our church finds value in Bible-based devotions and a practice of gratitude and that they only have time for this work on the weekends, then we shouldn't push an email newsletter during the workweek. Conversely, if we find that many of our congregants are commuters, we might seek to create a podcast reflection on the week's readings and preaching that's the duration of an average commute.

It's at this point in the conversation on hybrid ministry that many tend to give up. It's difficult enough to create equitable online and offline experiences. Promoting personalized, practice-based technologies seems like an additional burden, one that is unsustainable for the overextended church leader. It's only when we've thought about the practices our community values and the space they might have for such

87

practices that we can select the technologies that will fit our ministry context without additional investment or resources. When we think about tools and tech, we need to remember that less is more. We probably already have all the tools we need. Texting, email, and social media are often preferable to resource-intensive web or app development. Podcasts and digital video can be recorded, edited, and published with free software. And many church website services automatically include mobile websites, and perhaps even mobile apps, as part of their most common subscription models. In the hybrid church, we don't need to become software engineers. We just need to know what tools we have access to and how we can match those resources to spiritually edifying practices. In the hybrid church, we don't need to become prolific content creators. We just need to be purposeful about taking the prayers, preaching, and practices that are already part of our ministry and integrating them into a week in the life of our church community.

The ability to equip people for service is the key strength of in-person church community. When we use personalized, practice-based technology, we extend this ability into digital spaces. When we integrate the church's life with individual faith practices, we create an environment that consistently uplifts the church body for service and discipleship—on Sunday mornings and in every moment of the week. That's fundamentally what practice-based technologies are designed to do: not to replace the in-person church, not to jettison the strength of synchronous church community or to eliminate the need to gather as one, but to unify the communal with the personal. These tools are not individualistic, self-help resources like those so common in secular spaces. Though these resources may be personalized, they are always calling us back to where the Word is proclaimed and the sacraments administered. They are always returning us to church community.

A COLLABORATIVE CULTURE

When we bring together a parity of experiences with personalized, practice-based technologies, we establish a foundation for being church in a new way. With these practices, we can become a collaborative community, one where all contribute to the mission, where we all actively serve as the hands and feet of Christ. Enacting this commitment to collaboration is the goal of all hybrid ministry and the core of the Digital Reformation.

In the digital age, a collaborative church culture is characterized by clearly articulated pathways to involvement. When we create a parity of digital and analog experiences, we offer pathways to involvement in the mission of the church that are available to all. Whether someone is a longtime member or a first-time visitor, whether they are connecting online or sitting in the pews, they know exactly how to use their gifts in service to the mission of the community. When we equip for ministry using personalized technologies, we learn that our involvement is meaningful, that our service emanates from our calling as disciples of Jesus Christ.

So many churches, in an effort to align with our broader tech-shaped culture, talk about becoming collaborative. In fact, collaboration was one of the four cultural values identified in *Grace and Gigabytes*. In that book, I described how our digital technology is replete with collaborative tools and that our most widely used tools encourage tech-shaped culture to be increasingly collaborative. Resources from Google Docs to Microsoft Teams lead us to expect opportunities to contribute when, where, and how we would like—including in the church.

But while churches can and should adopt collaborative frameworks and shared leadership models, we cannot become collaborative simply by talking about it or even by deploying the right tools. We cannot arrive at more collaborative forms of ministry through leadership frameworks and ministry models. Collaboration is our goal, but it is difficult to actualize in and of itself. In fact, the best way to become collaborative is to start with a focus on hybrid ministry. The degree to which we welcome and support online connections illustrates our commitment to collaboration. The extent to which we invest in and equip our communities through service via personalized practices reveals how much we value shared leadership. Collaboration, thus, is the result of a thoughtfully planned hybrid ministry. It is the product created when we build a bridge between the online and the offline. Our ability to become a collaborative church first depends on our ability to fully implement hybrid ministry.

Becoming a hybrid church is a worthwhile yet difficult endeavor, a challenge I recognized on Easter morning 2021. As I had predicted, that Easter was indeed different from Easter 2020. While the pandemic continued, cases had abated to a point where it was safe to gather for socially distanced outdoor worship. With the sun shining brightly on a splendid spring morning, my family and I drove to worship in person for the first time in thirteen months, joining nearly two hundred others from the church under a white rental tent in the asphalt parking lot.

The burgundy chairs, brought out from the sanctuary, were spread across the parking lot, placed six feet apart in front of a makeshift altar and mobile lectern. Orange extension cords stretched into the church building, supplying electricity for microphones and speakers. Boxes that had once held bulletins now contained extra masks and hand sanitizer. Ushers who once passed collection plates across the aisles stood beside an offering box near the entrance to the tent. A poster with a QR code invited those gathered to download a digital bulletin, available via Google Docs.

When I arrived, the pastors were eager to greet every-one, to welcome them back to church. The church staff had begun the day with an outdoor daybreak service before moving inside for an online, livestreamed service that was also broadcast on local television. Once that ended, they went back outside for the "big" service with hundreds of attendees, including local news cameras, to broadcast a story of life returning to "normal." To my surprise, they didn't look like church leaders who were about to begin their third worship service of the morning, the sixth in the last three days. Despite how fatiguing that morning must have been to clergy, staff, musicians, and other volunteers, though, being back together, face-to-face, buoyed everyone's energy levels.

It was a mostly traditional Easter liturgy, though some aspects were new. It was the first worship service for which I accessed a bulletin on my smartphone, the first service when we were encouraged not to sing the hymns. But just as that morning felt new, it felt familiar: the traditional hymns, the familiar readings, the people we had worshipped alongside on countless previous Sundays.

As we departed that morning, we were invited to take a "to-go" Communion cup. With concerns over the safety of communing with nearly two hundred individuals during a pandemic, the pastors had spoken the Words of Institution over prepackaged wafers and grape juice. Walking toward our car, we received the elements, which we would eat and drink from the safety of our own parked vehicles. Eating the bread and drinking the wine in a parking lot that was occupied by so many, I was grateful for all the work that had gone into creating that Easter morning worship, that experience of a return to normalcy. As I took Communion while wearing a seat belt and waiting for the parking lot traffic to clear out, I was grateful, knowing that though our community may have changed, we were still called together to be the church, still blessed by the grace and goodness of God. We weren't taking Communion by intinction or through a common cup. We weren't celebrating the meal in the same room, nor were we hearing the words "given for you" spoken directly to us. But we were celebrating the Lord's Supper, tasting the reality of God's goodness, remembering that we belong to a perennial tradition that is ever shifting and evolving.

Taking Communion that Easter morning in the front seat of our 2011 Chevy Equinox was just one of the many aspects of that community that had been altered based on the reality of the pandemic. Many of the specifics of our life together had changed temporarily; some aspects had changed permanently. Nonetheless, I was grateful to be gathered into that community, however much it may have changed. Setting the empty container in the cup holder beside a lukewarm cup of coffee, I joined the line of cars turning out of the church parking lot, driving off into the brilliant sunlight of that Easter morning.

Yet driving away from church that morning, I recognized that the transition to hybrid ministry would require considerable time and energy from church leaders and ample flexibility from Christian communities. Having noted the busy morning of the pastors, musicians, and church staff, I realized that for all we might talk about the Digital Reformation, there will always be a sense that being present online requires a doubling of efforts—that we will feel at times like it requires twice as much work as gathering as the analog church. Having seen the reaction of those who were returning to church, even if only to the parking lot, I recognized that most of our community will desire a return to in-person community and will have little energy or enthusiasm for digital.

Hybrid ministry presents the greatest change management challenge ever experienced in the contemporary church. Many of us won't even attempt to make the transition. Those of us who do will find ourselves stymied by limitations on resources, time, and energy, to say nothing of those who oppose in principle the church's presence in digital spaces. Having established parity of experience and practice-based technologies as the defining attributes of hybrid ministry, therefore, we turn now to its implementation. Despite the obvious challenges, how can we recognize the promises of hybrid ministry as the digital age accelerates? As it turns out, the future of the hybrid church may depend less on our technological skills and more on our ability to accompany and coach our communities through both small changes and significant transformation.

THE FIRST DAY BACK

SUSTAINING HYBRID MINISTRY

The congregation had reserved a bounce house. After a phone call with a local party rental company, the church had secured the inflatable castle for its "Re-Rally Day," intended to be the largest in-person event since March 2020. At 8:30 a.m., the party rental company would inflate the bounce house in the church's suburban parking lot, where it would stand next to a rented petting zoo, a dunk tank, and a live music stage. While past rally Sundays had been intended to gather the congregation on the second Sunday in September for its first fall worship, this Sunday would be about more than sign-up sheets and Sunday school. The church had placed ads in the local newspaper promoting the event and started an ad campaign on social media. They even developed a website specifically to build awareness and enthusiasm. It would be a day of celebration. Even the church's Covid-19 task force—comprised of distinguished local physicians, university immunologists, and area business leaders—agreed: by the second Sunday in September, it would be time for all to return to the church as we understood it before the pandemic.

And then the case numbers increased, little by little and then in sharp daily gains. The Delta variant of the coronavirus had emerged in the community. Health and safety precautions returned to area churches. The county restored its mask mandate. The church still held its Re-Rally Day event, but the sense of celebration was clearly muted. Only one child could use the bounce house at a time. There would be no petting zoo. And lunch would be served in grab-and-go containers. Due to an ambiguous sentence in the county's latest mask mandate, preachers in the area that Sunday even had to wear masks from the pulpit, as if to provide a visible sign that the digital distribution of the pandemic was far from over. Those who hoped to return to church as it once was must have felt a mix of disappointment and resignation on that day, which fell so short of initial expectations. The lingering pandemic would continue to cause widespread stress and untold suffering.

As I walked through the parking lot that Sunday, I noticed that young families with children still too young to be vaccinated were not in attendance. Nor were the elderly, who likely saw the concerning increase in cases and decided to remain at home. In their absence, I was reminded that the church's online presence extends an invitation to all of those who cannot gather in person, during a pandemic or in a time of relative cultural stability. And in that moment, I returned to the idea that the Digital Reformation is not a specific response to an event but an effort to achieve a level of inclusivity that will benefit the church well after the worst of the pandemic has passed. There will always be a reason a congregation cannot rally together at a specific time, regardless of how much effort we invest in communicating or even marketing that moment. Bounce houses and live music may attract some to an event at a church, but they are no match for pandemic illness, nor are they sufficiently enticing to overcome the demands of an overbooked schedule, the appeal of a weekend road trip, or simply a quiet weekend morning without anywhere to be. We might not have been able to jostle in a line with other sweet tooths, eager for cotton candy that Sunday morning, but there were still plenty of connections to be made. There was still a community to gather with, a gospel to proclaim, and a message to carry forth into a hurting world.

AN ADAPTIVE CHALLENGE

The Digital Reformation needs leaders with an aptitude for change management. As we live into the greatest change to church community since the Protestant Reformation, we need to accompany our communities as we collectively navigate this transition.

Church communities often struggle with inertia and can tend to snap back to the status quo ante whenever a transition is poorly or passively facilitated. Without attending to the transition to hybrid ministry, we are likely to revert to digital expressions of church that create a second-tier experience for virtual participants, one where digital connection is available but only as an alternative to in-person gathering. In this "back-row" experience, online participants might be able to passively watch worship or listen to a discussion, but the community does not actively facilitate their involvement. Or worse still, we may revert completely to prepandemic digital disconnection, unplugging from the hybrid norms of our tech-shaped culture. In this scenario, we not only forget all we have learned about church community during a time of physical distancing; we also become less inclusive of those who cannot participate in the analog church.

Churches need leaders with strong change management skills as we navigate our tech-shaped world but not just because some congregations can be change averse. With all the transitions congregations have endured since March 2020, even the most obstinate communities have demonstrated agility and flexibility. The main reason we need to practice effective change management is that hybrid ministry is more than a technical response to the short-term challenges associated with the pandemic.

Yes, it would be easy, and convenient, to think about hybrid ministry as a reasonable response to a temporary challenge. Digital forms of church community met a specific need during a finite (though prolonged) pandemic when churches were unable to gather due to Covid-19. According to this widespread thinking, hybrid worship and other aspects of the Digital Reformation are technical fixes, or what Ronald Heifetz and Donald Laurie describe as "technical adjustment within basic routines."[1] We see digital ministry as a one-off challenge, an opportunity that can be addressed once before turning to the next significant need. Digital ministry seems to be only an add-on to the church we have always known, something worthy of investment and energy but not requiring that we reimagine core community practices and day-to-day routines. If digital ministry is merely an add-on, it does not require us to challenge beliefs about the structure of church community or to rethink our values that might give shape to a certain way of being church.

The problem with thinking about digital ministry as a technical add-on is that it confines digital ministry to its own silo within the congregation, independent of other aspects of a community's life. If we think about digital ministry as a solution to a technical challenge, we are likely to delegate it to those with technical skills and a sufficient degree of media savvy. This line of thought precludes the integration of the online and the offline that is essential to the hybrid church. It also prevents active collaboration across the congregation. If digital ministry is the work of a small set of technical experts, those in our communities without expertise in streaming technologies and digital content creation are unlikely to see the virtual as an authentic expression of church community.

The Digital Reformation is not a technical change, nor does it require exclusively technical solutions driven by media or communications professionals. It is what Heifetz and Laurie define as an adaptive challenge, or work that challenges deeply held beliefs and calls into question our values. Adaptive challenges, according to Heifetz and Laurie, "are often systemic problems with no ready answers."[2] They are challenges that call us to question our deeply held beliefs in order to thrive in new environments. Only when we approach and sustain hybrid ministry as an adaptive response to a broad, long-term challenge, a strategic move for ministry in uncharted territory, can we practice effective change management. Hybrid expressions of church may have become more common since the Covid-19 outbreak, but the purpose and value of digital church community will extend well beyond a time of social distancing. As Jim Keat, digital minister at the Riverside

Church, remarked on an episode of the *How We Do Digital Ministry* podcast, "Digital ministry is not a vertical silo in the church. It's a horizontal slab that covers every single thing. What is the digital ministry of worship? Of stewardship? Of education? Of pastoral care? Of social justice. It must be embedded in all of them."[3]

The challenge of being a hybrid church in a changing culture is most certainly an adaptive challenge, defying easy solutions. Tod Bolsinger describes leadership challenges that push us well off the familiar map in his book *Canoeing the Mountains*. The movement toward hybrid church community surely moves us into uncharted territory.[4] The Digital Reformation calls for what Bolsinger defines as "communal transformation for mission," facilitating "the transformation of a congregation so that they, *collectively*, can fulfill the mission they, *corporately*, have been given."[5] Or as Heifetz and Laurie say, charting a path to a solution to an adaptive challenge requires "the collective intelligence of employees at all levels," who collaboratively learn their way to new methods for a changed landscape.[6] They state that as with any adaptive challenge, the work of the leader is to "challenge current roles and resist pressure to define new roles quickly."[7] In the Digital Reformation, we are tasked with engaging ideas and expertise across our communities, resisting the tendency to see that the leader's ideas are the ideal solutions. The road map toward Digital Reformation is about far more than adding new software and hardware to our technology stack. The challenge for leaders is to keep our communities engaged, facilitating dialogues and sharing ideas, so that we, collectively, can adapt and thrive in a new environment.

When change is navigated collectively, the broader community is invested. When change is imposed by an individual atop an organizational chart, the broader community may be informed, but they may not be motivated to assist with its implementation. In an environment where leadership turnover is constant, where competing priorities and demands on our energy are relentless, efforts driven by the vision of a single leader may take flight, especially as followers' energy flags and falters when the individual leader moves on to the next challenge. Collective effort is required to drive sustainable transformation.

BEGINNING WITH PURPOSE

When we understand the movement to hybrid ministry as an adaptive response requiring collective action, we might recognize the need to inspire our communities to contribute to the transformation. The work of inspiring and rallying our communities requires articulating a broad purpose, then matching individual involvement to individual sentiments about the change.

Leadership expert Simon Sinek explores how to rally organizations in support of transformation in his book *Start with Why: How Great Leaders Inspire Everyone to Take Action*. Contrasting leaders who succeed in bringing about change with those who fail to motivate their communities to act, Sinek concludes that leadership in times of change is fundamentally concerned with purpose. For Sinek, leading through change isn't about communicating the specifics of what is changing but is instead about articulating the reasons driving a change. Organizations that collectively navigate transformation share

THE HOLY AND THE HYBRID

a widely known and agreed upon sense of purpose. Employees, members, or stakeholders within these organizations, whether they are businesses, nonprofits, or churches, are keenly aware of the driving purpose behind a major change. With a shared understanding of the reasons driving a change, members of these organizations are more likely to contribute ideas, share feedback, and actively contribute toward all that is changing.

Conversely, members of organizations that fail to implement lasting change might know what is changing, but they don't know why. They can list that which is about to be transformed, but they don't perceive a reason for the transformation. Without this level of shared understanding, these individuals are less likely to make constructive contributions in support of the transition. They may become passive or even opposed to the change. A church cannot become hybrid unless individual members understand the purpose and importance of a new approach to community. As leaders, we must define these reasons before we get far along with the tools and technologies used by the digital church.

The Purpose of Hybrid Ministry Is Not Technology

Though this book is about the Digital Reformation, the purpose of this change actually has little to do with technology or digital media. Hybrid ministry, after all, is a method or technique. As a way of doing church, it is a "how." It is not a purpose in and of itself. Streaming technologies, social media feeds, and digital offering plates are also not a purpose. They are merely tactics or tools. They are a "what." They are resources, but they are not reasons for transforming the way we do church. Methods and techniques, tactics and tools, seldom motivate whole communities to change, particularly in communities that tend to be somewhat change averse. This is a particularly crucial distinction in conversations about hybrid ministry. Few people, if any, are interested in the hardware and software, the literal and metaphorical nuts and bolts of online church. We come to church for an experience of the transcendent, not to compare and contrast technical tools and their suitability for ministry. If we lead through this change by focusing on hows and whats, we are unlikely to create a lasting hybrid community that is invitational and equipping.

Some of us tend to imagine that the purpose of technology has something to with growth. This is somewhat paradoxical: many of our churches shifted online in March 2020 to try to preserve some semblance of Christian community throughout digital distribution, yet when we think about the future of the church online, we think about not survival but acceleration. You've undoubtedly heard such sentiments. If we stream our services, create great content, and show up on social media, then our church will certainly grow. When we do these things, surely we will establish new and enriching connections with neighbors near and far! Though this reasoning is widespread, it has some limitations. Namely, it commodifies our digital connections. If the purpose of virtual church is growth, then virtual participants are simply fuel for that growth. Focusing on increased numbers can hinder the establishment of authentic relationships.

Another line of thought suggests that the purpose of hybrid ministry is innovation. According to this reasoning, we need to shift online because dwindling numbers and resources demand change ("What we've been doing isn't working, so we have to do something, anything, different"), and the internet is a logical setting for such efforts. When we think about the purpose of hybrid ministry as meeting the need to change and innovate, then we are likely to be disappointed. The Digital Reformation is not an antidote to all that ails our institutions. It will not balance a shrinking budget sheet or simplify a bureaucratic organization chart. Focusing on innovation, or institutional longevity, unmoors us from the core aspects of Christian community that we must work to preserve: public worship, preaching of gospel, and administration of the sacraments.

The Purpose of the Digital Reformation Is Inclusivity

In many conversations I have had about the Digital Reformation, leaders have lamented their lack of technical skills. Without the necessary digital aptitudes, these leaders cannot see themselves leading through this transformation. I encourage them to let go of the what and how (plenty of skilled people and resources are available) and instead to focus on the why—the real leadership issue and the anchoring purpose of this reformation: the inclusive proclamation of the gospel. The purpose of hybrid ministry is not about church growth or Christian innovation. It is instead about the inclusive proclamation of an unchanging gospel to a rapidly changing, tech-shaped culture. The Digital Reformation, rightly approached, is more about continuity than change. Rather than replacing the foundation of the church, or Word and sacrament, we are simply working to make Word and sacrament accessible where our communities are to be found. In some sense, then, the Digital Reformation is more about transposing church to a new key, one better suited for new environments. The shift is more subtle than radically remaking church.

We can see how digital technology leads to inclusivity when we examine some of the specific attributes of hybrid ministry. By creating bridges between online and offline participants, we mitigate certain barriers to inclusivity that pervaded the analog church. We aren't just creating inroads with "digital natives" or opening the doors of church to those who work on Sunday mornings, however. We address the barrier to an inclusive gospel proclamation that results from disability. The physical ability to travel beyond one's home is a privilege enjoyed by some but not all. In church circles, those who are unable to easily leave their home have often been referred to as "shut-ins." While the term has been used to organize and manage ministry practices such as visiting and bringing the sacraments to those who are ill, the label is problematic. It implies that in a sanctuary, within a building, *we* worship. At your house, where you are homebound, *you* wait for an able-bodied minister to come to you. It suggests that at this time and in this place, we experience grace. At another time and in another place, you receive the leftovers. Even as the term "shut-in" has been replaced by words like "homebound" or phrases like "those with disabilities," those who are disabled and temporarily able-bodied are treated as separate communities within a congregation.

During the Covid-19 pandemic, many of us stayed home far more often than we had been accustomed to, choosing not to travel to places with large crowds because it was unsafe to do so. While these months of social isolation were challenging, perhaps it made us more empathetic toward those who, for their own reasons, do not leave their homes. Perhaps one of the improvements we made during the pandemic was to eliminate the artificial and problematic hierarchy between "worshippers" and "shut-ins." The Digital Reformation is a movement toward becoming a more inclusive church. When we build bridges between the online and the offline, we're eliminating a potential source of bias within our church community, erasing the value judgments about those who do not participate in the life of the congregation in person.

While we as church leaders might support the purpose of hybrid ministry, we may not see its specific potential in our low-tech ministry contexts. When we begin to talk to our communities about hybrid ministry, we should clarify that this journey is not just for those with media teams, IT budgets, and high-speed internet connections. Hybrid ministry doesn't require media budgets, production teams, or investments in hardware and software. The Digital Reformation doesn't necessitate sound and video editing or an IT staff. We're not seeking to become online televangelists with the reach of a Joel Osteen. Rather, any ministry can live into the Digital Reformation by working toward inclusivity. We're simply looking for the best way to connect communities through the work of the Holy Spirit and send them into the world to love and to serve their neighbor.

Ultimately, our digital resources and technical skills do not determine our capacity for hybrid ministry. Rather, it is determined by our willingness to proclaim the gospel beyond our sanctuaries, even unto the ends of cyberspace. This anchoring purpose will always matter more than the particulars of a congregation's information technology.

ORGANIZING AROUND PURPOSE

After we communicate the purpose for a new way of being church, we will inevitably encounter three categories of responses from our faith community. To lead effectively, we must differentiate among these brackets, which are based on the Rogers diffusion of innovations theory, a conceptual framework explaining how communities adopt new technological processes and practices. It theorizes that adoption of or engagement with new technologies can be plotted on a bell curve;[8] that is, that people fall into somewhat predictable categories and can be expected to respond in particular ways. Early adopters are eager to test new technologies and processes and often take responsibility for leading and advocating for the change. The majority may not fear change, but they want to understand the purpose or see the value before committing to an idea.[9] Only a small group, fewer than one in five, will resist the change.

Leading the way through the Digital Reformation requires us to listen to each of these three groups and to get them involved in the ongoing transformation. Effective leaders recognize the needs and gifts within each of these segments of our church community rather than attempting to create the hybrid church through top-down change. By identifying, affirming, and engaging early adopters, the majority, and laggards alike, we ensure that our hybrid ministry remains a collaborative, sustainable ministry. Our opportunity as faith leaders will be to involve the early adopters as advocates; to convince the majority that the change is valuable and appropriate, so they become connectors; and to accompany the laggards through their initial resistance.

Innovators and Early Adopters

The transformation to hybrid ministry begins by inspiring and involving the supporters, by harnessing the enthusiasm some will have for this change. As with any organizational change, we can expect that approximately one in five members will be clear advocates. Known in the change literature as innovators or early adopters, this approximately 15 percent slice of our congregation represents a small yet significant portion of the organizational change curve.[10]

When leading through any change, we must build on this group's enthusiasm. Hybrid ministry is no exception. According to marketing expert Seth Godin, author of many books on change and innovation, the implementation of any new idea depends on successful engagement with the advocates, the innovators, and the early adopters. According to Godin, those who launch new services or models mistakenly focus on the masses who have comparatively little enthusiasm for the new idea. For Godin, bringing a new idea, product, or service to the majority is likely to end with widespread apathy or indifference. But it is the advocates who influence the broader community, who will promote the change with those who are neutral or somewhat resistant to the idea.[11]

Godin wasn't writing for pastors, but his ideas are relevant to hybrid ministry. Applying this concept to the Digital Reformation is simple: we must begin by creating leadership roles for those who already support the transition to digitally integrated ministry, because their support and involvement will ultimately determine if we succeed in building a bridge between the online and the offline. And although we have few documented best practices for hybrid ministry, we ought to involve them in imagining the ideas that are best suited for a particular ministry context. When this group is involved in this work of ideating and brainstorming, they are more likely to share the story and impact of digital ministry with the rest of the community.

The question, then, is how do we identify the early adopters within a faith community? Some of the early adopters will be found among the select few who have a passion for A/V technology and assist with running church media. But the early adopters in a congregation include more than our media techs. In your church community, there are likely many individuals who find it difficult or frustrating to connect with the analog church. The Sunday morning in-building experience is challenging for families with young children. The trip to the sanctuary can be tedious or time consuming for those with mobility challenges. The homogenous demographic composition of most mainline Protestant worshipping assemblies can be frustrating for young, single individuals, people of color, and the LGBTQ community. Those who are challenged by the early morning start time, frustrated by the buildings' lack of accessibility, and skeptical of the church's lack of authentic diversity are likely to be advocates of hybrid ministry. Some of them will be young "techies." Some will be elders who have rarely, if ever, used a computer.

Overall, our early adopters are likely to be a highly diverse community who will share in a commitment to making the community more inclusive. This group will ultimately determine whether we create a bridge between the offline and the online or the online becomes a "back-row" alternative to in-person forms of community. Accordingly, leaders in the church shepherding the Digital Reformation will want to get them involved from the start. Their involvement will tend to fall within three categories: design, production, and communication.

The designers are those who will help us figure out the specific shape of hybrid ministry in their context. These are the supporters of the change who have a gift for discernment, for thinking about how the inclusive purpose of hybrid ministry aligns with worship, education, fellowship, and service. Designers may be individuals who were quite active in the prepandemic church community and who have a keen awareness of both its challenges and opportunities. The designers don't need to determine where to put the camera or how to create a media team volunteer schedule. But they will be willing to explore the specific opportunity that hybrid ministry presents in their context. With their efforts focused on the early side of the journey to hybrid ministry, we should bring together the designers in a retreat-style conversation, to discern and to dream big about the church's digital future.

The production people are supporters who have specific gifts and aptitudes for digital technology, those who might volunteer to run the tools and technology. They set up the livestream, host video conference discussions, and test out new software. They may even teach others how to connect to the church online, demonstrating how to use a church app or navigate a church website, for example. Not all churches are blessed to have early adopters with a passion for production, so a production team might connect with students who are studying technology or communications.

Finally, the communicators are those who are willing to talk to others about why hybrid ministry matters. This group would be tasked with communicating why inclusivity matters to them personally—and how they see hybrid ministry as supporting these objectives within the church. While they may not have the same discerning mindset as the designers or the "techie" mindset as the producers, they have a story they want to share and a gift for telling it. They are likely to be members of the community who have some credibility with the group, who are willing to speak up in support of inclusivity and accessibility, willing to put themselves out there to share why this change matters. With a topic as abstract and often as uninteresting as "technology in the church," we need stories that humanize the journey to hybrid ministry, that will lead to a shared experience of empathy. Through blogs, videos, newsletters, presentations, or lay preaching, the communicators will have an ongoing, prophetic role within our community: broadening our understanding of what it means to be invitational, leading us into new ways of connecting. Returning to Simon Sinek's advice, it is the communicators who empower us to "start with why," who move the conversation from the technical and the abstract toward the human and the concrete.

As I noted above, one in five or six members of our community is likely already an advocate of hybrid ministry, an innovator or early adopter not because they love tech but because they believe in the purpose. By identifying this slice of the community, we identify where the transformation begins. As we engage with planners, producers, and communicators, we ensure that our digital experiences of church will remain as real and as human as anything experienced within our walls. When this work begins, it builds momentum, increasing the likelihood that the majority of our community will learn to contribute to church in ways that are emerging and potentially unfamiliar.

The Connectors

Most in our church community will be neither advocates nor resisters of technology in the church. As with any change or transformation, this majority—the connectors or the early and late majority—will likely include supporters of the status quo, those who are just fine with the church we are, and those who would find it acceptable to test new approaches on occasion. The early and late majorities are willing to try new ways of doing church; they just don't want to be the first to try them. They're willing to be part of an innovative ministry so long as someone else leads the way. Because they represent over half of any community, our efforts to become digitally integrated depend on the majority testing digital connection, on participating in virtual worship, joining a class or meeting through video conference, using a church app or website, or contributing to a conversation through social media.

With a somewhat indifferent opinion of technology in the church, these connectors likely won't have much interest in the work of planning, production, and communication. While our primary task with the advocates was to involve them in a process of shared leadership, our primary task with the majority of our congregation is to persuade them to adopt the change. We want them to see the value of hybrid ministry and to try connecting to the community online. The more connectors we can convince to engage online, the more fully that hybrid ministry will be integrated into our church culture.

Church leaders and hybrid ministry early adopters should talk to the connectors about hybrid ministry in three ways: articulating the purpose, sharing the story, and communicating the details. The connectors need to hear the purpose and, from time to time, to hear the stories of how that purpose is concretely making the church more inclusive by making it more accessible.

While we don't need to verbalize that purpose in every communication or at every worship service, having a pastor or other established church leader periodically explain the church's specific call to the Digital Reformation ensures that we sustain the bridge between the online and the offline and retain the support of the connectors. We can also visualize or restate the purpose at the specific entry points to digital community—with signage near cameras and video conference setups, with descriptions on our websites, with reminders in newsletters and bulletins. The more we can contextualize our digital tools and tactics within this sense of accessibility, the more likely our connectors are to reimagine the faith community as a hybrid of the online and offline.

Despite these efforts, the majority of our congregation still may not want to connect to their faith community online. But if we navigate this change effectively, they will understand why online matters to the congregation's life together. They will see the specific value of accessibility. They'll hear the personal stories about why hybrid ministry matters to real people. And they'll recognize that they will have the opportunity to join in the church's digital life together, when and if they choose to. Ultimately the test of how well we have led the connectors through this transformation is less about "usage" and more about attitudes, less about data and more about understanding. We shouldn't concern ourselves with the frequency of this group's participation in digital spaces. But we should care about whether they see virtual as an authentic expression of Christian community, as the location of real ministry with real people.

The Resisters

The resisters (sometimes known as "laggards") will be easier to identify than the connectors or the advocates. As with any change, they will make their opinions known from the start. Anecdotally, many pastors have struggled with church leadership councils composed primarily of the change averse. We need to attend to the resisters because they likely will at times occupy leadership positions or have outsized influence on the congregation and may control our ability to invest in a digitally integrated ministry.

Hybrid ministry detractors may not resist everything about the Digital Reformation. Having seen the importance and value of some online church community throughout the pandemic, resisters are unlikely to want to unplug completely or to argue that the church has no place in digital spaces. More likely they will be ambivalent. The resisters may support creating only an online "alternative," placing a camera at the back of the sanctuary and livestreaming a worship service, for example. If asked to share their opinion, they will argue that the online is a less desirable form of community and that there is no need for parity between the analog and digital. Failing to accompany this slice of our congregation increases the likelihood that digital integration will become an afterthought, that passive consumption rather than active engagement will define the church's presence in digital spaces.

While we want to engage the advocates and communicate with the connectors, our approach to the resisters centers on listening. We need to talk to these individuals and listen to their concerns. Their pushback likely comes not from an opposition to hybrid ministry but from a fear that the church they once knew will never return to "normal."

Perhaps the best way to begin talking with and listening to these individuals is not to ask for their opinions about the use of technology in the church. We don't need to give them an outlet for complaints. Instead, we should ask them to think about the future of the church. We might ask them to consider the exclusivity of conventional ministry models in a culture where 50 percent are no longer church members, where 30 percent work on Sunday mornings, and where our culture's spiritual landscape is changing faster than ever. We might gently remind them that without becoming more inclusive and accessible, entire Christian denominations are likely to disappear within our lifetime.[12]

Then we should ask them to think about who we are called to be and what God is calling us to do. In other words, we should ask them to reflect on our church's mission. If we get too technical with these conversations, if we get stuck on "what we do" instead of "why we do it," we are unlikely to get anywhere. But if we invite the resisters to reflect on the future of our ministry and how we can sustain our shared sense of connection and service for another generation, we may find that we're all more willing to change than we might expect.

We don't need to persuade all the resisters. We may not even need to persuade any of them. We simply need to show up for the conversation, to share why we think hybrid ministry matters, to invite reflection on where God is calling us next. All changes in Christian communities have their detractors.

Resistance is inevitable. If we show up to listen, empathetically and sincerely, our conversations may be enough to sustain the bridge between the online and offline once it has been established. This isn't a conversation about cameras near the pulpit, presence on social media, or computers in the narthex, all of which tend to provoke surprisingly strong opinions from resisters. This is a conversation about our future, about whether all that is great about our church community will be accessible to those who most need the church, about whether it will be available to a new generation.

SUSTAINING OUR EFFORTS

Even with the guidance of experienced leaders of change, the process is challenging. So how do we care for ourselves during this transformation, ensuring that our efforts and energy are sustainable? With digital integration pushing church leaders to test new approaches and adopt new technologies, we are traveling a steep learning curve, which will at times drain our energy and reduce our focus on more traditional aspects of church leadership. Even in the best of times, leading a church can be depleting, even if the calling is fulfilling.

Before the pandemic, thousands of ministers were leaving ordained ministry—and in some cases the church—each month, and that was before we had to reinvent the foundational structure of communal life. With 90 percent of pastors working an estimated fifty-five or more hours each week,[13] we should be concerned about the leadership costs intrinsic to the Digital Reformation. Indeed, we cannot be both pastor and producer at the same time. Vicar and videographer are two separate professions. However we implement hybrid ministry in our context, we cannot expect ourselves or our congregations to do more. So how do we manage this transition in an environment where resources are already constrained, where staff are constantly overworked, and where new ideas often struggle to gain traction? I would propose three commitments that will serve us well throughout the transition: purposefulness, iteration, and minimalism.

If we approach digital integration with a focus on the tactics and to-do lists, hybrid ministry becomes just another task on an endless checklist. It becomes a source of constant internal frustration and likely a cause of fruitless comparison to other churches. Approached as a to-do list, hybrid ministry may not be manageable. There will always be more to do, more tech to add, more tools to spend resources on. This approach will inevitably lead to dissatisfaction and burnout. We'll see what other churches are doing, how they are creating parity of experience, how they are using technologies to equip, and we'll want to do the same, if not better. So we'll add their tactics and tools to our already too-long to-do lists. When we don't arrive at the same level of tech sophistication as our neighboring church, we'll wonder why we can't keep up and scold ourselves for our failure. We'll blame ourselves for not leading more effectively and our communities for not being "innovative."

Approached as a checklist, digital integration leads inevitably to exhaustion. Thus we should continuously return to the purpose of hybrid ministry. In response to God's call and mission, we seek to create a church that is more inclusive for all. In doing so, we can broaden our invitational reach and equip our communities for service. When we remain focused on the "why" instead of the "what," our efforts will become more sustainable. When viewed as a sacred purpose or even as a calling, leading into hybrid ministry becomes a joyful exercise in Christian leadership. It doesn't require vast additional resourcing to explore how a church can be incrementally more accessible.

Second, we should seek to remain committed to iteration, to regularly testing new approaches and exploring how a ministry setting can be most accessible. Part of the reason it's important to start with the "why" is that there is no one way to become a hybrid church. Freed from the checklist mentality, we can view digital integration as a continuous experiment. We're not trying to create a finished "product" or a technological "solution," even as we are working with technology. Rather, we are trying to align our method of being church community to a changing culture.

Practicing iteration in the Digital Reformation involves two processes: asking questions and testing ideas. If we fail to regularly ask questions of purpose and of sustainability, we are likely to exhaust ourselves on approaches to digital integration that don't align to our context. If we don't reflect often on these questions, we will be unable to cut the ideas that don't work for us. I recommend asking,

- What is the best, most sustainable way to make our congregation more consistently inclusive?
- What are we currently doing that is standing in the way?

Digital media in the church is a relatively new experiment. All tech in ministry should represent an idea about how we can be more purposefully inclusive. And as experiments and ideas, they can be stopped at any time. They can be reimagined and shifted, reworked and scaled back. They can also be expanded and solidified. Though some technologies involve contracts and licenses, we must never feel obligated to stay with an approach to technology that is inadequate or unsustainable.

In a ministry context, livestreamed worship is one experiment of how to create parity between the online and the offline. Blogs and podcasts are one possible tool for equipping individuals for service. Zoom calls and social media are another possible means of convening communities in digital spaces. The ubiquity of these technologies, particularly during the pandemic, might lead us to think of these approaches as permanent or essential. In fact, we should be constantly scrutinizing these tools. They are, in effect, just the tactics of the Digital Reformation, the "what" and the "how" of a new way of being church. We have the freedom and responsibility to shelve them or to try new ideas when testing suggests it is time to move on.

Finally, we need to remember that in the world of technology, less is often more. I'm a technology enthusiast, a former Google employee whose view of technology is more optimistic than many. But even I know that we in the church are not called to be technologists nor IT professionals. That's why I'm such a believer in Cal Newport's work on Digital Minimalism, the philosophy that we should use only the technologies that align with our purposes. To Newport and other digital minimalists, technology is a resource we can use in service to our values. We ourselves are not tools in service to technology! I am convinced that Newport's description of Digital Minimalism is beneficial to all of us during this time of transformation: "Digital Minimalism is a philosophy of technology use in which you focus your online time on a small number of carefully selected and optimized activities that strongly support things you value, and then happily miss out on everything else."[14]

This "less is more" standard is particularly important in areas of church leadership and administration. As faith leaders, our task isn't to use all technologies and apps at all times. Creating a collaborative environment conducive to shared leadership does not require us to use Slack, email, texting, Zoom, and Google Docs all at the same time, or even at all. Our calling is to be intentional about using the tools that enable us to invite and equip in pursuit of a more accessible, inclusive church. As church leaders, we should regularly reflect on the purpose of technology, constantly prioritizing and often eliminating what is superfluous or unsustainable.

Recognizing that those entrusted to us live in an online world and that many of these people are exploring faith and spirituality, we would be wise to not unplug completely. But without additional staff and volunteers, without new budget allocations for IT equipment and support, we'll need to be selective about where we plug in. Hybrid ministry, then, is a process of selective unplugging, of using the technologies that are most important as we form our communities for lives of faithful service.

The shortage of real-time collaborative tools has often limited the potential for shared leadership within the church. But that the work of the people can happen without constant digital distraction, without the digital addictions that often characterize the workday in high-tech industries, is a gift and a blessing that we should not relinquish. The key challenge is to utilize the least amount of technology possible that still allows us to work together for the sake of mission. The opportunity is to find the minimalist mix that helps us serve together synchronously and asynchronously, online and offline, from the building and from anywhere.

Being thoughtful about technology usage will benefit not just the busy pastor but all involved in a faith community. We seem to assume that individuals are attracted to high-tech churches. In fact, the opposite might be true. People are often looking for a retreat from the world of constant noise and ceaseless notifications. We serve them well when our technologies make it easier to connect to what's happening within the community or when they provide a source of spiritual sustenance. We do them a disservice when we impose too much tech, when the abundance of the online obscures God's grace that we hope to experience. As a member of my congregation recently shared with me, the more technology we add to our faith community's week-to-week events and operations, the more difficult it can be for members to connect. The more buttons one has to press, the more links one has to keep track of, the more tools one has to download, the less likely it is that an individual will stay involved in the church's life together.

Our communities still want to know Christ and to experience connection with one another. We should use no more and no less technology than we need to make this possible. But how do we know our use of technology is not optimized? Start by looking at elements that are duplicative or distracting. Our aim should be to create opportunities for meaningful collaboration. If technology is redundant and if it is burdensome, it is not worth using.

Of course, there is one other criterion: actual usage. Yes, we could simply eliminate the digital tools when there is little activity. For example, we could delete a seldom-viewed social media account or YouTube channel. But we should do so with some caution. Even a seldom-used app or resource can provide someone with a connection point to the congregation, offering a pathway to involvement in the life of the community. Therefore, before we remove technology in the name of Digital Minimalism, we should carefully scrutinize whether we are removing something that could help the church be more invitational—more accessible and inclusive—in the future, even if that resource is seldom used in the present.

When we overburden our faith communities with apps and hardware, subscriptions and services, we're that much more likely to revert to the analog church. In a hybrid ministry, less technology creates more connection—for ordained leaders, staff, and congregation alike. This sense of greater connection leads to more consistent inclusion. When we choose technology that enables us to gather, equip, and collaborate, our communities are more likely to embrace the church's digital future and to join in living into our shared mission.

THE NEXT STEP FORWARD

The Digital Reformation is a call to develop a more inclusive church. This is a summons to a great experiment that many church leaders are willing and eager to answer. Who among us wouldn't want to find ways to increase our invitational reach within a tech-shaped culture in order to meaningfully equip more individuals for lives of faithful service? Who among us wouldn't want to deconstruct barriers that prevent those entrusted to us from hearing the gospel message?

Conversely, only a few of us are innately interested in discussions about online worship, digital faith formation, and tech-supported leadership. That's why it's so important to lead through this transformation with a keen sense of purpose. If we can do that, we expand this conversation beyond the tedious aspects of technology that tend to inhibit dialogue on the church's hybrid future. Ultimately, leading through the transition and accompanying our communities through its unique challenges should be a joyful and faith-enriching endeavor.

Though the Digital Reformation presents one of the greatest leadership opportunities of our times, it also presents one of the greatest change-management challenges. Faced with the need to transform from an analog to a hybrid model, tasked with redefining what it means to lead a ministry, we will at times experience stress, if not outright burnout. The challenges will create self-doubt. And the self-doubt will call into question the very value of digital integration, particularly if we stray from the purpose of this work. The more we focus on the what and how and the more we drift from our why, the more disenchanted we will become. We might, therefore, ask the question, What if technology is bad? More specifically, what if technology is a distraction to Christian communities rather than an asset? It is to these questions we turn in the final chapter.

CAMPFIRE WORSHIP

*THE LIMITS AND OPPORTUNITIES
OF HYBRID CHURCH*

I first felt a call to serve the church while working as a camp counselor. I served for two summers at Pine Lake Camp in Waupaca, Wisconsin, a 120-acre site populated, predictably, with a dense Eastern White Pine forest. The camp, a part of Crossways Camping Ministries, primarily serves Lutheran congregations in Northeast Wisconsin. Many of these churches send their entire confirmation class for a full week at the start of every summer. While some campers alternate nights at camp with Little League games and volleyball practices, most of the seventh through ninth graders stay Sunday through Friday. What they experience in those five nights, separated from their cell phones and school friends, is unlike anything that they experience at their home congregations. Through some Bible study and acoustic-guitar-driven worship, but mostly through informal conversations and shared meals, they connect with one another. They learn one another's stories; they come to recognize how God is at work in their lives. Far from the lure of screens and messaging apps, the campers come to the woods to hear a different type of calling.

Each year, the counselors design an introspective Light Service for the last night of the week. Traditionally a quiet and contemplative conclusion following days of high-energy activity, the service might feature skits and dramatizations one year, songs and stories another year. The Light Service my first summer on staff focused on a theme of silence.

It began at the lakeside campfire circle, a small amphitheater adjacent to the swimming area. As the sun would set each Thursday, two counselors paddled a canoe from the middle of the lake, lighting a tiki torch as they slowly beached the canoe near the fire circle. One of the counselors, typically our lifeguard, would step out of the canoe and read a passage from Deuteronomy: "Then Moses and the Levitical priests said to all Israel, 'Be silent, Israel, and listen! You have now become the people of the Lord your God'" (Deut 27:9 NIV).

As the lifeguard proceeded up the stairs of the amphitheater, the campers were invited to follow the path to the candle-lit chapel, stopping occasionally to listen to messages from the camp staff on the importance of silence and stillness in the journey of faith.

Just as the procession of middle school youth and college-aged staff neared the log cabin chapel, a historic building sitting atop the camp's highest hill, they would stop to listen to one additional reflection, usually read by Cyle, a camp counselor who is now a software engineer.

"Do you have an iPod?" Cyle would ask.

"Two iPods? Do you have a cell phone?" he would continue, starting his reflection with a list of the most popular consumer technologies from 2008.

"Why do we so eagerly add all of this noise to our lives," he would ask, "when all of this noise makes it so difficult to hear the voice of God?"

As the doors to the chapel opened and the sound of the guitar echoed off the log cabin walls, the campers were given a few quiet moments to look back on their week at camp, to reflect on where they had seen God at work, to think about how that might change their lives after the drive home.

And so each week of that summer, I was reminded that technology can be a distraction. If we're not careful, it can crowd out any opportunity for sacred silence and stillness. If we're not mindful of our phones, our computers, and our internet usage, they may overpower the voices that we most need to hear.

THE LIMITS AND OPPORTUNITIES

For the most part, our digital ecosystem is morally neutral, a place that is morally what we make of it. When we enter into an online space, we can bring our best selves and our worst selves. We can engage those on the other side of the screen with empathy, remembering that they are created in the image of God. Or we can dismiss others online as insignificant, even nonhuman, reducing them to a screen name or an avatar.

As a member of a generation formed from birth by digital technology and as a decade-long contributor to leading tech companies, I'm inclined to view the world of tech positively.

I've seen how digital tools bring us together: how messaging apps unite families across vast distances, how social media preserves friendships that would have otherwise drifted throughout the years, and how business apps foster collaboration and inclusivity among peers. But even I sometimes grow skeptical of technology's presence in the church. Having experienced vibrant Christian community in intentionally low-tech settings such as campus ministries, retreat centers, and summer camps, I sometimes wonder whether technology is needed to carry out our mission or is simply another attempt at cultural relevance. Sometimes this skepticism turns toward discouragement. After learning how social media groups and online misinformation catalyzed the January 6, 2020, attack on the United States Capitol, I worry that technology, social media in particular, might do real harm to our communities.

When I do feel skeptical or worried about the encroachment of tech into faith communities, I inevitably return to Martin Luther's idea that we are all simultaneously saint and sinner—both redeemed and fallen. Digital spaces, like all other spaces, reflect the truth that we are a creation blessed by God from the very beginning yet simultaneously living with the realities of brokenness. Digital spaces are a product of the best and the worst of human nature. They can reflect brokenness or blessing, support division or unity, tear down or build up. We are broken, *and* God considers us righteous. Through Christ's life, death, and resurrection, Jesus has overcome the forces that draw us away from God. The forces of commodification, misinformation, and polarization are ultimately powerless in light of Christ's redemptive and liberating work in the world, including cyberspace.

The Limits

The more consequential problems that technology causes our society are well documented. But it's not just the highly visible issues of social misinformation or teen cyberbullying that reveal the brokenness in our technologies. The brokenness we see on the web doesn't affect just young people, however, nor is it caused only by bad actors. All of us can utilize tech in ways that contribute to brokenness. For example, while online, all of us, no matter how well intentioned we may be, are vulnerable to context collapse,[1] digitally oversimplifying the nuances of everyday life into truncated text and overedited images. Digital communication lacks the interpretive cues that are so useful for fully contextualizing the purpose and meaning of face-to-face interaction. Social media in general, Instagram and Twitter in particular, facilitate context collapse for both creators and viewers of digital content. When we post to social media platforms like Twitter or Facebook or send a message through platforms like Snapchat, we can't know for certain who will read our message, how they will interpret it, or how they might react. Social media and digital messaging also prevent recipients from understanding the expectations and values of those whose messages we view.

Context collapse is problematic for several reasons. On the less harmful end of the spectrum, it can lead to simple miscommunication. When we don't fully understand the context of those who will read our messages and posts, we more easily fail to express ourselves in ways that will meet readers and viewers where they are, so our thoughts may be misconstrued. More significant, we might post a message that turns out to be callous, crass, or even offensive to our social media circles.

Often, these situations arise when we make assumptions about the composition of our digital media circles, when we assume our Facebook friends all have similar political views or that our coworkers have similar tolerances for crass humor or that everyone on a work email thread is likely to share the same opinions. Context collapse makes communication, and trust, more difficult, presenting challenges for those who would like to cultivate intentional digital community.

Context collapse also contributes to digital misinformation, the sharing of information that is not just factually inaccurate but distorted to advance particular and often partisan interests—to privilege an individual or benefit a specific group at the expense of another. While misinformation is obviously a challenge in our political affairs, Christian circles are hardly immune to the problem. Many Christian circles contain content that is not only dishonest but incomplete at best, one-sided and biased at worst. A particularly churchy form of misinformation involves those who create online Christian content and engage in proof texting, selecting out-of-context verses in an effort to share the "biblical" view of complicated cultural issues in order to gain influence and followers. While this problem of misinformation isn't unique or new to the internet, the speed with which misinformation can be spread and the lack of accountability to a tradition or an established community makes the problem especially egregious. Overly simplified or maliciously inaccurate content on complex issues spreads simply because it garners likes, retweets, and shares. Further, some supposedly Christian online content isn't even Christian. According to *Relevant Magazine*, nineteen of the top twenty pages identified as "Christian" on Facebook at the time the research was conducted were run not by churches but by

Eastern European "troll farms," groups dedicated to manipulating users into clicking ads, revealing personal details, or disclosing confidential information to hackers or other bad actors.[2]

At times, this process of oversimplifying, distorting, and deceiving is simply an attempt to "win" online arguments on contentious topics. As we reduce the life of faith to a series of biblical jabs and theological uppercuts, we come to view Christian community not as a place of collaboration but as a source of contention. As Jay Y. Kim, lead pastor at WestGate Church in California's Silicon Valley, writes in his book *The Analog Church: Why We Need Real People, Places, and Things in the Digital Age*, "We've become skilled at making fast-paced, quick-hit points and winning arguments. The problem is, meaningful community is forged slowly, over time, with much compromise and understanding. Healthy communities invite nuance and emphasize reflective responses over rash reactions. Real connections within real communities are realized only as we walk together down the path of wisdom, not cleverness."[3] As church leaders, we sometimes contribute to the worst within online spaces when we seek to win arguments rather than convene community-wide conversations. As the divisiveness of the political sphere continues to expand its influence over our culture, we need to choose wisdom over cleverness and invite conversations with thought-provoking questions rather than ending them with definitive answers.

But context collapse and the spread of misinformation can be fairly mundane issues when contrasted with issues that cause physical and psychological harm. When I think about the worst of the web, I think about 6:15 p.m. on Wednesday evenings. That's when confirmation class has traditionally started at my church. When I've taught for our program, 6:15 p.m. is a moment of abrupt transition. This is the moment when the students are asked to put their phones away. Seventy percent of all American teenagers send and receive messages with Snapchat, a mode of messaging that is now as prevalent as texting.[4] For many, 6:15 p.m. means temporarily stepping away from Snapchat, putting aside their "streaks," or streams of constant back-and-forth communication.

At that moment, though, I'm actually less concerned about whether the students are using their phones or messaging on Snapchat and more worried about the messages some are receiving through these channels. While these apps often create and sustain friendships, which is why so many are drawn to them, they also have a tendency to create a perpetual sense of FOMO, "fear of missing out." FOMO has been defined as a "pervasive apprehension that others might be having a rewarding experience from which one is absent," an apprehension that is widespread on social media. According to researchers, FOMO starts with viewing posts and photos from connections that appear to depict fuller, more rewarding experiences than we ourselves have access to in a given moment. This continuous exposure to depictions of supposedly better experiences than our own in turn leads to lower self-esteem and even to depression, anxiety, and social media addiction.[5] Facebook's own researchers seem to have reached similar conclusions. An October 2021 article from the *Wall Street Journal* detailed how employees at Instagram found that using Instagram, known for its easy image-editing features, is harmful for a sizeable percentage of Instagram users, particularly for teenage girls.[6]

FOMO is just one of many problems in the social media world. But FOMO is less overtly harmful than cyberbullying.

Research shows that among youth, Snapchat, used by more than 70 percent of American teenagers, is one of the internet's three busiest platforms for incidents of cyberbullying.[7] Cyberbullying is an often unseen form of marginalization that affects one in every five teenagers.[8] At times, the weary and anxious facial expression of a student sitting apart from the others serves as a reminder that cyberbullying is prevalent, perhaps even more rampant than we could imagine. While cyberbullying has some differences from bullying that takes place in the physical world, its consequences can be just as severe. Individuals who are cyberbullied are at risk for depression and even suicide. These effects become particularly severe when a teen experiences simultaneous cyber and physical forms of bullying.[9]

Congregations are unlikely to add to the significant brokenness of digital technology. The risk isn't that church leaders will somehow become propagators of misinformation or FOMO. But there is a risk that increased use of digital technology in ministry may increase exposure to the brokenness of these systems. Prayers and blessings posted to Instagram may appear beneath the airbrushed and distorted images that cause FOMO and anxiety in the first place. Facebook may harvest data from a congregation's conversations on Facebook in order to serve ads and profit off personal data and user attention. Services streamed to social media sites may increase time spent on the site, increasing the likelihood that someone clicks an ad or views content that is manipulative or deceitful. The entrapments of exposure are unlikely to dissipate, even as digital platforms crack down on their various ailments. Still, I believe we are called to do ministry in these spaces, to form Christian community and to offer a Christ-like presence in them. For all its problems, digital technology provides us with the tools to be a blessing. Approached thoughtfully, these tools will bless our communities far more than any possible harm technology may cause.

The Opportunities

Indeed, technology can be bad—for our communities and for us as individuals. Still, I am reminded of instances when I experienced considerable social good through Christian community online. I think about CaringBridge pages where friends and family connect to pray for a loved one with a chronic illness or volunteer to run errands. I think about GoFundMe efforts that have raised thousands of dollars to support a community member facing mounting medical bills. I'm reminded of the seminary student Facebook groups that mutually support one another through the rigors of theological education and a call to a ministry vocation or the church Facebook pages that connect refugees to job listings and even furnishings for their new homes.

But the blessings of digital faith community extend beyond general social goods. Each of these online communities provides a forum where we can live out our baptismal commitments: to live among God's faithful people, to learn the Scriptures, to be nurtured in faith and prayer, to proclaim Christ through word and deed, and to work for justice and peace. When we join an online page or group for our congregation and contribute to conversations occurring in these spaces, we are living among God's people on more than just Sunday morning. When we share photos and occasions for celebration or name the longings and losses we are experiencing within those communities, we are connecting in a way that reminds us that Christ and our Christian community are with us in both joy-filled moments and our darkest days. We can learn the Scriptures and study what it means to live a life of faith in this digital age through church blog posts or podcasts. Better yet, when we contribute to the creation of that podcast or blog post, we are creating and collaborating, joining as active contributors to the story of God's reconciling work in our world and proclaiming Christ in word and deed. When we share and respond to prayer requests on social media, email, or text messaging, we are supporting one another through faith and prayer. Even the simple practice of noting a prayer request on a social media news feed, pausing, and lifting that concern up to God supports our own faith development, as it nurtures the needs of the community through prayerful support. And when we join a virtual book discussion, show up for a volunteer or service event that was organized online, or contribute time and treasure to a valued cause, we are doing the work of justice and peace.

Indeed, as challenging as digital community can be, the web is full of faith-filled spaces centered on the life, death, and resurrection of Jesus. Our digital world provides an abundance of tools for teaching the Scriptures, apps for nurturing prayer and other spiritual practices, spaces for supporting one another through the ups and downs of life, and connections to individuals and communities who will serve us and offer us opportunities to serve. For every story of digital misinformation, for every experience of social media shaming or trolling, there is a story of a community coming together online as the people of God to love and to serve. For all the instances of division on the web, there are stories of how digital tools facilitate the deepening of our relationship with God and the nurturing of Christian community. For all the times that the web leads to isolation, there are moments when these spaces are connecting us in rich new ways that allow us to share our story and to hear how Christ is active in our lives. When we become a hybrid church by integrating the analog with the digital, we present our communities with an opportunity to question and to connect, to collaborate and to create, to be a hybrid church, a community that is a blessing to all who participate.

AN ENDLESS ROAD

After my second summer as a camp counselor, I started a different kind of job, trading the Waupaca woods for the walls of a cubicle and an ever-noisy job in the technology industry. Now when I look back on that Light Service, the contrast between those quiet moments in the log cabin chapel and the tech world I'm immersed in today sometimes makes me wonder if the Digital Reformation is, as it seems, leading us on the road to distraction, misinformation, and fractured relationships. Yes, it's important for all of us, when thinking about the church's presence in digital spaces, to retain a healthy amount of skepticism about its centrality to our communities. Technology can certainly be distracting, dividing, and destructive. It can indeed crowd out the voices of loved ones and especially God's call for our lives. Amid such doubt and uncertainty, I sometimes wonder if the gifts of the analog church were made possible by the church's relative distance from digital spaces. Could it be that the analog church's propensity for trusting relationships, vulnerable and open dialogue, and commitments to service are made possible by the church's relative distance from digital spaces?

But then I remember the many ways in which tech can be a source of immense blessing. It can connect us to voices and perspectives we need to hear. It can help us reimagine our call to love and to serve. It can help us discover what it means to practice Christian discipleship. I remember that the Digital Reformation does not draw us away from the community and conversations that were supported by the analog church. Rather, it draws us deeper into those commitments as we seek to preserve them for a digital age. The Digital Reformation beckons us to establish uplifting community online, to be a continuous source of digital blessing.

I travel back to Pine Lake Camp nearly every chance I get, usually not to attend a formal program or retreat but simply to be on a site that has such sacred meaning in my life. I always appreciate walking through the woods or strolling along the beach, even as recent higher water levels have eroded much of the shoreline. I always value my conversations with those I meet on site: the staff, the camp directors, the volunteers. I am especially grateful that even today my cell phone does not work on the property. The tall forests appear to block my phone's 5G, and the camp office's wireless internet remains just slow enough that it's not worth connecting to.

Like so many ministries, the camp was forced by the coronavirus to close in summer 2020, which meant restrictions on visits and gatherings. Still, all that is good and holy about this ministry remained available to Pine Lake campers, staff, supporters, and staff alumni not through the woods but through digital community. Site directors made videos of the changing seasons and filmed virtual tours of site projects, sharing to

Facebook Live and Instagram. Summer staff read children's books, sending recordings to the region's congregations to be used as children's sermons. Former staffers posted "Throwback Thursday" photos to a Facebook page for past counselors, sharing black-and-white pictures of summer nights from decades ago. And when the decision was made to reopen at 50 percent capacity in summer 2021, supporters gathered on Zoom for a virtual trivia-night fundraiser, raising money to purchase health and safety supplies for the coming summer. The pandemic did not stop the ministry of Pine Lake Camp or Crossways Camping Ministries, nor did it prevent those who have been blessed to be a part of this community from carrying on with the work of service and discipleship.

My hope is that the woods and waters of Pine Lake Camp will always be available to me, to my family, to my church. It's undoubtedly a sacred place where all are invited to experience the goodness and graciousness of God. It's a place that silences the distractions in our lives, centers us within embodied and intentional community, and creates a space for honest and empathetic conversation. In doing so, it attunes us to the voice of God.

Yet we learned in 2020 that camp is not a place that's bounded by lines on a property map or by dates on a program calendar. Camp is a ministry community, a meeting of disciples who have been called by the Holy Spirit and formed into one for connection and service, regardless of geographic location. More than ever, I need this ministry in my life. Thanks to the Digital Reformation, Pine Lake is more accessible than ever.

With hybrid ministry, the work of the people joined together as the church becomes limitless. We continue to gather face-to-face in order to form and equip our communities. We connect digitally in order to extend the broadest possible invitation to an encounter with Christ. The teachings and connections that equip us for lives of faithful service become more widely accessible. By extension, living a life of discipleship becomes increasingly plausible. The grace and mercy of God emanate from our sacred sanctuaries, radiating outward to create disciples in a digital age, commissioned to heal a hurting and divided world.

The question for us as leaders, then, is not whether technology can be used for good or for bad, for helpful collaboration or for hurtful communication. It can clearly be used for both. Nor is the question whether church technology will be a source of connection or distraction. It can be used for either. The question is how we as church leaders will show up in these spaces. Knowing that digital spaces allow us to extend an inclusive invitation to an encounter with Christ, how will we be present in such a way that makes them more incarnational and gracious? Knowing that face-to-face connections are crucial to equipping individuals for discipleship, how will we continue to cultivate offline community? Leading into the Digital Reformation demands that we reimagine our ministries as a hybrid of online and offline. We do this work not only for our faith communities, for our own members, but for those who might not know the peace and joy of God's grace. When we do this work well, we demonstrate to the digital world what it means to be a disciple—at church, in our neighborhood, and on the web. When we do this work intentionally, the church can teach a hurting world what it means to be fully human. With our efforts, our digital spaces become more inclusive, our communities more dedicated to service. Through our work, the web can even become sacramental, a place where the real presence of Christ is made known.

Notes

Preface

1 Tod Bolsinger, *Canoeing the Mountains: Christian Leadership in Uncharted Territory* (Downers Grove, IL: InterVarsity, 2018), 15.

2 Elizabeth Drescher, *Tweet If You Heart Jesus: Practicing Church in the Digital Reformation* (New York: Morehouse, 2011), 4.

Chapter 1: The Last Coffee Hour

1 Anne Holcomb, "Families Who Travel Long Distances to Attend Church Are Led by the Spirit, Family and Friends," MLive, January 17, 2009, https://www.mlive.com/living/kalamazoo/2009/01/_louie_and_franny_silva.html.

2 PNW Conference, "How Churches Spend Their Money," *Pacific Northwest UMC News* (blog), December 2, 2014, https://www.pnwumc.org/news/how-churches-spend-their-money/.

3 Robert Wuthnow, "Religious Involvement and Status-Bridging Social Capital," *Journal for the Scientific Study of Religion* 41, no. 4 (2002): 669–84.

4 T. Claridge, "Social Capital and Natural Resource Management: An Important Role for Social Capital?" (unpublished thesis, University of Queensland, 2004).

5 Joanna Maselko, Cayce Hughes, and Rose Cheney, "Religious Social Capital: Its Measurement and Utility in the Study of the Social Determinants of Health," *Social Science & Medicine* 73, no. 5 (September 2011), https://www.ncbi.nlm.nih.gov/pmc/articles/PMC4169277/.

6 Pippa Norris and Ronald Inglehart, "Religious Organizations and Social Capital," *International Journal for Non-profit Law* 6, no. 4 (September 2004), https://www.icnl.org/resources/research/ijnl/religious-organizations-and-social-capital.

7   Maselko, Hughes, and Cheney, "Religious Social Capital," 759–67.

8   Robert D. Putnam, David E. Campbell, and Shaylyn Romney Garrett, *American Grace: How Religion Divides and Unites Us* (New York: Simon & Schuster, 2012), 469.

9   Putnam, Campbell, and Garrett, 451.

10 Putnam, Campbell, and Garrett, 469.

11 Putnam, Campbell, and Garrett, 492.

12 "Religious Landscape Study among Members of the Evangelical Lutheran Church in America (ELCA)," Pew Research Center, 2014, https://www.pewforum.org/religious-landscape-study/religious-denomination/evangelical-lutheran-church-in-america-elca/.

13 See the 2019 and 2020 results for the American Time Use Survey at "American Time Use Survey," US Bureau of Labor Statistics, accessed November 23, 2021, https://www.bls.gov/tus.

14 "Choosing a New Church or House of Worship," Pew Research Center, August 23, 2016, https://www.pewforum.org/2016/08/23/choosing-a-new-church-or-house-of-worship/.

15 Tristan Claridge, "What Is Bridging Social Capital?," Social Capital Research, January 7, 2018, https://www.socialcapitalresearch.com/what-is-bridging-social-capital/.

16 Robert D. Putnam, "Social Capital Primer," Robert D. Putnam, May 23, 2017, http://robertdputnam.com/bowling-alone/social-capital-primer/.

17 Putnam, 174.

18 "In U.S., Decline of Christianity Continues at Rapid Pace," Pew Research Center, October 17, 2019, https://www.pewforum.org/2019/10/17/in-u-s-decline-of-christianity-continues-at-rapid-pace/.

19 "In U.S., Decline."

20 R. J. Reinhart, "Religious Giving Down, Other Charity Holding Steady," Gallup, December 21, 2017, https://news.gallup.com/poll/224378/religious-giving-down-charity-holding-steady.aspx.

21 Alex Conrad, "10 Powerful Church Statistics on Social Media Use," MinistryTech, May 25, 2018, https://ministrytech.com/social-media/10-powerful-church-statistics-social-media-use/.

22 Paul Steinbrueck, "The Shocking Percentage of Churches That Still Don't Have Website," *Christian Web Trends* (blog), January 9, 2015, https://www.ourchurch.com/blog/the-shocking-percentage-of-churches-that-still-dont-have-website/.

23 Ella Koeze and Nathaniel Popper, "The Virus Changed the Way We Internet," *New York Times*, April 7, 2020, https://www.nytimes.com/interactive/2020/04/07/technology/coronavirus-internet-use.html#:~:

text=But%20a%20New%20York%20Times,for%20work%2C%20play%20and%20connecting.

24 "Percent of Population Who Worked on Weekdays and Weekend Days," Bureau of Labor Statistics, American Time Use Survey, accessed November 23, 2021, https://www.bls.gov/tus/charts/chart11.pdf.

25 "State of Play 2020: Pre-pandemic Trends, Ages 13–17," Aspen Institute Project Play, 2020, https://www.aspenprojectplay.org/state-of-play-2020/ages-13-17.

26 Vicki Salemi, "76% of American Workers Say They Get the 'Sunday Night Blues,'" Monster Career Advice, accessed November 22, 2021, https://www.monster.com/career-advice/article/its-time-to-eliminate-sunday-night-blues-0602.

27 Ellen Edmonds, "AAA Forecasts Americans Will Take 700 Million Trips This Summer," AAA Newsroom, June 25, 2020, accessed November 13, 2020, https://newsroom.aaa.com/2020/06/aaa-forecasts-americans-will-take-700-million-trips-this-summer/.

28 Hannah Sampson, "What Does America Have against Vacation?," *Washington Post*, August 28, 2019, https://www.washingtonpost.com/travel/2019/08/28/what-does-america-have-against-vacation/.

29 Lori Ioannou, "A Snapshot of the $1.2 Trillion Freelance Economy in the U.S. in the Age of Covid-19," CNBC, September 15, 2020, https://www.cnbc.com/2020/09/15/a-snapshot-of-the-1point2-trillion-freelance-economy-in-the-us-in-2020.html.

Chapter 2: The First YouTube Baptism

1 ELCA Office of the Secretary, "Tracking Online Worship Attendance," Evangelical Lutheran Church in America, accessed October 25, 2021, http://se-email.brtapp.com/files/documents+%26+brochures/files/tracking+attendance+resource+042020.pdf?fbclid=IwAR1QStcqhdFDaWwRF2zN-Pb8jgSqPZl0_FqDarPtjMJiXcy8QF2lcH5goJw.

2 Barna, "What Research Has Revealed about the New Sunday Morning," State of the Church 2020, June 3, 2020, https://www.barna.com/research/new-sunday-morning/.

3 Barna.

4 Barna.

5 Claire Gecewicz, "Few Americans Say Their House of Worship Is Open, but a Quarter Say Their Faith Has Grown amid Pandemic," Pew Research Center, April 30, 2020, https://www.pewresearch.org/fact-tank/2020/04/30/few-americans-say-their-house-of-worship-is-open-but-a-quarter-say-their-religious-faith-has-grown-amid-pandemic/.

6 Nadia Bolz-Weber (@sarcasticlutheran), "Sunday Prayers," Instagram photo, March 14, 2021, https://www.instagram.com/p/CMZ23YUnHMM/.

7 Brené Brown (@brenebrown), "Church Is Back!," Instagram Live, March 22, 2020, https://www.instagram.com/p/B-DGh6eJVIQ/?hl=en.

8 Alan Cooperman, "Will the Coronavirus Permanently Convert In-Person Worshippers to Online Streamers? They Don't Think So," Pew Research Center, August 17, 2020, https://www.pewresearch.org/fact-tank/2020/08/17/will-the-coronavirus-permanently-convert-in-person-worshippers-to-online-streamers-they-dont-think-so/.

9 Cooperman.

10 "Religious Congregations in 21st-Century America," National Congregations Study, 2015, accessed November 15, 2021, https://sites.duke.edu/ncsweb/files/2019/02/NCSIII_report_final.pdf.

11 "Music Became Even More Valuable on YouTube in 2019," Pex, accessed February 2, 2022, https://pex.com/blog/state-of-youtube-2019-music-more-valuable/; Pamela Bump, "40% of People Say They Don't Read Blogs: Here's How You Can Still Get on Their Radar," Hubspot, March 23, 2020, last modified March 26, 2020, https://blog.hubspot.com/marketing/do-people-read-blogs.

12 Ryan Holmes, "Are Facebook Groups the Future of Social Media (or a Dead End)?," *Forbes*, October 29, 2108, https://www.forbes.com/sites/ryanholmes/2018/10/29/are-facebook-groups-the-future-of-social-media-or-a-dead-end/?sh=748940e31d23.

Chapter 3: The Next Easter

1 Cooperman, "Coronavirus."

2 Rachel Pelta, "Is Remote Work the Future of Work?," *FlexJobs* (blog), accessed November 2, 2020, https://www.flexjobs.com/blog/post/future-of-remote-work-stats/.

3 Susan Lund et al., "What's Next for Remote Work: An Analysis of 2,000 Tasks, 800 Jobs, and Nine Countries," McKinsey & Company, March 3, 2021, https://www.mckinsey.com/featured-insights/future-of-work/whats-next-for-remote-work-an-analysis-of-2000-tasks-800-jobs-and-nine-countries.

4 Lund et al.

Chapter 4: The First Day Back

1 Ronald A. Heifetz and Donald L. Laurie, "The Work of Leadership," *Harvard Business Review*, December 2001, 7, http://cpor.org/otc/Heifitz(2001) TheWorkOfLeadership.pdf.

2 Heifetz and Laurie, 8.

3 Jim Keat and Christopher Harris, "Virtual Isn't the Opposite of Physical," Faith Growth, streamed on November 1, 2021, YouTube video, 34:24, https://www.youtube.com/watch?v=uufowKKbsj8.

4 Bolsinger, *Canoeing the Mountains*, 17.

5 Bolsinger, 40.

6 Heifetz and Laurie, "Work of Leadership," 6.

7 Heifetz and Laurie, 9.

8 Evan T. Straub, "Understanding Technology Adoption: Theory and Future Directions for Informal Learning," *Review of Educational Research* 79, no. 2 (2009): 625–49.

9 John-Pierre Maeli, "The Rogers Adoption Curve and How You Spread New Ideas throughout Culture," Political Informer, September 10, 2018, https://medium.com/the-political-informer/the-rogers-adoption-curve -how-you-spread-new-ideas-throughout-culture-d848462fcd24.

10 Andy Swan, "How to Spot Companies Accelerating through the Adoption Curve," *Forbes*, April 12, 2020, https://www.forbes.com/sites/andyswan/ 2020/04/12/how-to-spot-companies-accelerating-through-the-adoption -curve/.

11 Seth Godin, *Purple Cow: Transform Your Business by Being Remarkable* (New York: Penguin, 2002), 17.

12 Dwight Zscheile, "Will the ELCA Be Gone in 30 Years?," FaithLead, September 5, 2019, https://faithlead.luthersem.edu/decline/.

13 Molly Rossiter, "Pastor Burnout: Who Helps the Helpers?," *Gazette*, February 13, 2015, https://www.thegazette.com/community/pastor-burnout -who-helps-the-helpers/.

14 Cal Newport, *Digital Minimalism: Choosing a Focused Life in a Noisy World* (New York: Penguin, 2019), 28.

Chapter 5: Campfire Worship

1 Jessica Vitak et al., "'Why Won't You Be My Facebook Friend?' Strategies for Managing Context Collapse in the Workplace," ACM Digital Library (paper presented at iConference '12: Proceedings of the 2012 iConference, Toronto, Ontario, February 2012), 555–57, https://doi.org/10.1145/ 2132176.2132286.

2 Tyler Huckabee, "In 2019, Almost All of Facebook's Top Christian Pages Were Run by Foreign Troll Farms," Relevant, September 28, 2021, https://www.relevantmagazine.com/culture/tech-gaming/almost-all-of -facebooks-top-christian-pages-are-run-by-foreign-troll-farms/.

3 Jay Y. Kim, *The Analog Church: Why We Need Real People, Places, and Things in the Digital Age* (Downers Grove, IL: InterVarsity, 2020), 91.

4 Werner Geyser, "Snapchat Statistics and Revenue: Snapchat by the Numbers," Influencer Marketing Hub, April 30, 2019, https:// influencermarketinghub.com/snapchat-statistics-revenue/.

5 Daria Kuss, "Mobile Technology and Social Media: The 'Extensions of Man' in the 21st Century," *Human Development* 60, no. 4 (2017): 141, https://www.jstor.org/stable/26765167.

6 Georgia Wells, Jeff Horowitz, and Deepa Seetharaman, "Facebook Knows Instagram Is Toxic for Teen Girls, Company Documents Show," *Wall Street Journal*, September 14, 2021.

7 Sara Harrison, "Teen Love for Snapchat Is Keeping Snap Afloat," Wired, July 23, 2019, https://www.wired.com/story/teen-love-snapchat-keeping -snap-afloat/.

8 Hillary K. Grigonis, "1 in 5 Teenagers Are Bullied Online, New Cyber- bullying Statistics Suggest," Digital Trends, July 22, 2017, https://www .digitaltrends.com/social-media/cyberbullying-statistics-2017-ditch-the -label/.

9 Evelina Landstedt and Susanne Persson, "Bullying, Cyberbullying, and Mental Health in Young People," *Scandinavian Journal of Public Health* 42, no. 4 (2014): 393–99, http://www.jstor.org/stable/45150813.

Recommended Resources

Books

Elizabeth Drescher. *Tweet If You Heart Jesus: Practicing Church in the Digital Reformation*. New York: Morehouse, 2011.

Drescher's book coined the term "Digital Reformation." The book is a thought-provoking exploration of the ways social media is changing the nature of relationships.

Keith Anderson and Elizabeth Drescher. *Click2Save Reboot: The Digital Ministry Bible*. New York: Church Publishing, 2018.

Anderson and Drescher's updated work is the definitive guide to building digital Christian community. Featuring diverse examples of online communities, the book offers a broad exploration of the social and digital media landscapes.

Michael Adam Beck and Rosario Picardo. *Fresh Expressions in a Digital Age: How the Church Can Prepare for a Post-pandemic World*. Nashville: Abingdon, 2021.

The authors explore how digital spaces have become the new third space and thus a missional frontier.

Dave Daubert and Richard E. T. Jorgensen. *Becoming a Hybrid Church*. Self-published, 2020.

In one of the first books on hybrid ministry, Daubert and Jorgensen explore the tactics and transitions involved with hybrid church. Their book includes a useful discussion guide for church boards and other planning groups.

Jay Y. Kim. *Analog Church: Why We Need Real People, Places, and Things in the Digital Age*. Downers Grove, IL: InterVarsity, 2020.

Kim provides a thoughtful critique of digital ministry, identifying the limits of online church community and questioning whether digital technology is capable of forming disciples.

Deanna A. Thompson. *The Virtual Body of Christ in a Suffering World*. Nashville: Abingdon, 2016.

A digital skeptic finds strength and support through digital community while undergoing cancer treatment. Thompson's story is a nuanced exploration of technology in Christian communities and a useful companion for change-averse congregations.

Podcasts

Be Still and Go with Jim Keat

A leading example of a congregation podcast, created by the Riverside Church in New York City. With over eleven seasons, *Be Still and Go* effectively integrates Scripture, story, and practice in a brief and accessible format. https://www.trcnyc.org/bsag.

Gospel Beautiful with Michael Chan

Focuses on stories of innovative ways to proclaim the gospel in an ever-changing world. Episodes in 2022 on hybrid ministry explore the opportunities and limitations of digital expressions of church. https://podcasts.apple.com/us/podcast/gospel-beautiful-podcast/id1484416194.

How We Do Digital Ministry with Christopher Harris
A weekly show featuring expert interviews with insights on tactics and tools. Many of the guests represent small- to medium-sized mainline congregations that have found creative ways to build digital community without large media budgets. https:// podcasts.apple.com/us/podcast/how-we-do-digital-ministry/ id1561971725.

Digital Communities

How We Do Digital Ministry Facebook Group
A companion to Christopher Harris's podcast, the group includes conversations on the tactics of hybrid ministry. Join the conversation at https://www.facebook.com/groups/ 712956465502081.
Luther Seminary Faith + Lead
A hub for courses and coaching on ministry trends and innovations. Since 2020, I have offered regular courses on ministry in a digital age, hybrid ministry, and the theology and ethics of online church. Sign up for a course or connect with a coach at https://faithlead.luthersem.edu/.
The Ministry in a Digital Age Newsletter
My weekly newsletter focuses on the trends, challenges, and opportunities in digital ministry. Subscribe at www .ryanpanzer.com.
Virginia Theological Seminary Lifelong Learning
Home to the eFormation conference, digital ministry office hours, and other learning experiences that focus on trends in digital ministry. Join the VTS mailing list for the latest information. For more, visit https://vts.edu/lifelong-learning/.